C000194946

TRENTHAM AT WAR

The story of a country estate during
World War II

Graham Bebbington
with a foreword by Sir Arthur Bryan

Published by

CHURNET VALLEY BOOKS

© Graham Bebbington 1995

First published 1995.
Reprinted 1998
Reprinted **2016**

ISBN 1897949 13 8

Printed and bound in the UK by 4edge Limited

CONTENTS

Foreword by Sir Arthur Bryan

Introduction
Acknowledgements

Chapter

Bibliography
Abbreviations

for
Lynne Margaret

Also by Graham Bebbington:

The Loggerheads Project   Newcastle Borough Council
Pit Boy to Prime Minister   University of Keele
A Brief Life   Isle of Wight County Press

Foreword

Reading Graham Bebbington's 'Trentham at War', readers will be transported to the Second World War fifty or so years ago. Stoke-on-Trent and the County gained much from the evacuation of the Banks from London and the Banks, for their part as they stated, gained also. The City's economy was uplifted in days of gloom and the cultural scene gained much. Friendships were forged and they continue; even marriages were bonded and locals and 'Outcasts' grew together during those grim years of war.

'Trentham at War' portrays many scenes of the period - evacuation of people, civic affairs, artistic events, charity appeals, tragedy and social affairs. A kaleidoscope of life at the time here in North Staffordshire. The author has a keen interest in people and this reveals itself in this wide review of our unique role in the war. Our community has long been proud of the contribution it made and still makes to our regiments, the Royal Navy and the Royal Air Force and this Trentham record should ensure our place in history as a generous receiver of the self-named 'Outcasts' from the Central Clearing House of the London Banks.

I am sure the banking community in London and the Bank of England will enjoy this generous review of their days at Trentham, Stoke-on-Trent, Staffordshire.

Arthur Bryan
24th January 1995

Trentham Hall, Staffordshire, seat of the Duke of Sutherland

Introduction

Much has been written about the Trentham Estate, Stoke-on-Trent - the former residence of the Duke and Duchess of Sutherland - and yet sadly, at this time, there is no concise history in print. However, the sole purpose of this work is to relate, as far as possible, the role of the estate during World War II and, in doing so, it confines itself to Trentham Gardens and Trentham Park.

Not only were the London Clearing Banks - the Central Clearing House or CCH - temporarily rehoused in Trentham Gardens during that period, a fact still not appreciated by many, but in addition Trentham Park itself was a major transit area for allied troops including, at one stage, a large number of that unique fighting force, the French Foreign Legion. Moreover, the estate was used variously for military training, a control point for prisoners of war, and convalescence of sick and injured British service personnel. It was also, on occasion, the location which happened to be a 'stepping stone' or a catalyst for important war-time operations. Consequently, Trentham's contribution to the allied cause should not be underestimated. In addition, the work illustrates the genuine bonds which were forged between people of different backgrounds, classes etc., because of the war, giving a cohension which is sadly not present today. No other attempt, to my knowledge, has been made to record this important period in North Staffordshire's history.

Whilst appreciating that there are a number of admirable books relating to the origins of the Second World War, I have nevertheless considered it necessary to refer briefly to the pre-war period to enable readers, hopefully, to appreciate the reasoning behind events which took place at Trentham.

Having said that, readers should also appreciate that this work does not claim to be a complete history of the period insofar as Trentham is concerned. Even 50 years after, barriers of official secrecy still shield aspects of the Second World War. Furthermore, times being what they were, there were occasions when an event was simply not recorded, curious as this may seem. There was, after all, a war on! Finally, one should also have regard to the fact that many of the Trentham Estate records for the period have been lost as a result of, amongst other things, water damage and inadequate preservation facilities. Those estate documents that are preserved are as a result, in particular, of the diligence of Bill Hoten, a former employee, and my own researches.

GB

We lived at last in a community with a noble common purpose and the experience was not only novel but exhilarating. We had a glimpse then of what life might be if men and women freely dedicated themselves, not only to their appetites and prejudices, their vanities and fears, but to some great communal task. We were, you see, better people than we thought.

J.B.Priestley.
BBC Radio 17th May 1945

Acknowledgements

I am especially grateful to Sir Arthur Bryan, not only for writing the foreword to this book, but also for the kind assistance and encouragement received from him and Lady Bryan during research.

In addition to those quoted in the text or source notes, I acknowledge most gratefully the assistance of the following:
A Cholerton CBE; Kay Priestley; the late Eugeniusz Lejman; Robert Fyson; Fred Bickerton; Jeanette Lawton of the British Deer Society; Richard A Durrant; Mrs N Smith; The Editor & staff of the Evening Sentinel, particularly John Abberley and librarian Andrew Hopwood; Fl. Lt. Joe Dean, RAF Stafford; Capt. P H Starling RAMC; P C Alan Lewis of the Staffordshire Police, C Ulph of the Paymaster General's Office; E W Stubbs, former Chief Inspector, The Clearing House; R C Anderson; Chris Salmon, Hon. Sec., Ceramic City Choir; Professor D Johnson, University College, London, and the Imperial War Museum, in particular Peter Simkins.

I am also deeply indebted to Dr Joan Delin for not only allowing access to research material for her doctorate on **"British Opinion and the French in Great Britain in 1940"**, Université Charles de Gaulle, Lille, but also for making valuable suggestions at the manuscript stage, and to John Grindey for designing the cover.

Special debts of gratitude are also due to my publishers, and in particular to Christine Pemberton for assistance and cooperation in producing this volume.

Finally, every endeavour has been made to trace source material. If, unwittingly, any copyright has been infringed, the author offers his apology and will correct any omissions in any subsequent edition.

GB

Central Clearing House, Trentham. *APACS*

Chapter 1
Preparations for War

'If Hitler had as many weeds in his garden as there in mine,
he would have something else to do!'

Observer in Evening Sentinel, 26th August 1939

During the summer of 1939 when war clouds loomed over the country, the people of Great Britain studied the news from Europe as one might survey the skies in an attempt to predict the weather. Journalists frequently used the term 'War clouds gathering' but it all seemed so far away. For the younger generation, in particular, with no painful memories of the First World War (the so called 'war to end all wars') life was carefree and fun, or so it appeared.

In any event, while Adolph Hitler was about to lay waste to Europe, many working class Britons were taking or preparing for their annual holidays. Not to be excluded, the 'blue bloods' were celebrating the regular social milestones - Royal Ascot, Henley Regatta, Cowes Week - with the usual zest. It was as if people generally preferred not to think of the possibility of hostilities but, on 3rd September, this air was abruptly shattered by Premier Neville Chamberlain's broadcast announcement of the declaration of war against Germany.

Throughout that summer the preparations for war had, in fact, began to intrude inexorably into everyday life. Ration books, identity cards and public information leaflets containing such advice as *'The protection of your house against air raids'* appeared. Buildings suddenly found alternative service as first aid posts etc., and in streets and gardens corrugated iron Anderson shelters and walls of sandbags became familiar sights.

Preparations for war had clearly began much earlier. As Harold Nicholson (later Sir) commented in The Listener on 14th September 1939 - *'We lolled and slouched into the First German War, the Second has found us infinitely more prepared.'* For example, in the early 1930's, against the threat of German re-armament, the British Government issued a specification seeking to replace outdated fighter aircraft. The result was R.J. Mitchell's Supermarine Spitfire. By early 1936 the prototype was ready and three months after its test flight the manufacturers received a £1.25 million order for 310 aircraft. By the outbreak of war 400 were in service. Incidentally, it was not only Mitchell's Spitfire which made a significant contribution to Britain's war effort but also his Supermarine Walrus, a bi-plane amphibian, which played a valuable role as the foremost fleet gunnery spotting and observation platform. One of the greatest aeronautical engineers, if not the greatest, Mitchell unfortunately died in 1937.

The threat of war resulted in activity in various quarters, some perhaps not so obvious to the general public. For example, whilst new factories were being built, or old ones re-equipped to reinforce the country's war machine, consideration was being given at Westminster to the powers that would be required to govern effectively, if hostilities commenced.

The result was the Emergency Powers (Defence) Bill, passed by both Houses of Parliament on 24th August 1939. Precise details of the measures were not, however, revealed at that stage, the presenter of the Bill, Home Secretary Sir Samuel Hoare indicating - *'We do not intend to introduce Regulations that would affect the liberty of the subject .... until the country is at war.'* He did, however, warn that the Government was seeking *'very wide, very drastic and very comprehensive powers.'* The question of such powers had, in fact, been under active consideration since 1935 when the Committee of Imperial Defence had set up a further Committee under the chairmanship of Sir Claud Schuster. Holding the post of permanent secretary to the Lord Chancellor, Schuster was instructed to devise emergency legislation that would be required in the event of war. The Committee's deliberations were extremely varied and included, amongst other things, imposition of curfews; instructions to manufacturers and farmers as to what they could produce; whether rare birds should be de-protected to enable their eggs to be consumed in times of food shortage; control of the country's finances; and a proposal involving internment of anyone *'whose detention appears to the Secretary of State to be expedient in the interests of the public safety or the Defence of the Realm.'* In effect, the resultant Bill enabled the Government to introduce whatever Regulations it desired and, within a short period of having received the Royal Assent, over 500 new laws placing restrictions on almost every aspect of life were introduced on to the statute book.

Whilst desperately hoping for peace, it was generally believed that if war did come the likelihood of enemy air attack could, for the first time, threaten the destruction of industry, commerce, communication and the whole organisation which the country relied upon to function and survive. Winston Churchill had, in fact, already written a paper on the subject in 1936.[1] The power of the modern bomber to influence wholesale slaughter and destruction had become an established fact, reinforced by newsreel photographs such as those of the Luftwaffe in 1937 bombing the Spanish town of Guernica. In addition, it was believed that war could inevitably involve the widespread use of poison gas which could saturate alike the streets of a city or the remotest valley. Thus it was decided that some evacuation would be necessary.

The question of war-time evacuation had, in fact, first been considered in 1931 by a Sub-Committee of the Committee of Imperial Defence. Its first report in 1934 advocated the evacuation of 3½ million from Central London to billets within 50 miles of the capital. However, following an increase in size of the Luftwaffe during 1936-7 and a realisation by military experts that any possible air attack would not necessarily be confined to the capital, it was decided that the whole question of evacuation required re-appraisal.

The subject was, in any event, to assume a new sense of urgency following the annexation of Austria by the Nazis in March 1938. It appeared then that war was inevitable. The assumption was also made by defence experts that war would commence with an immediate aerial bombardment by the Germans, not only of London, but possibly of other major cities as well. As a consequence, it was concluded that, to be effective, any evacuation had to be completed before bombing began, otherwise the operation would become disorganised or be of little practical value. More and more it began to be appreciated that Britain was no longer the island fortress. The stretch of water which, for centuries, had been the country's first line of defence could now be breached and appropriate evasive measures had to be taken, and urgently.

Whereas records appertaining to the revised evacuation scheme have survived, they are incomplete. This could be as a result of files having been heavily weeded or, alternatively, some documents never having been made public. Nevertheless, the skeleton of a scheme remains and can be appreciated from perusal of those papers which are on file at the Public Record Office. The plan, co-ordinated through a number of Government Committees, was impressive and the detailed arrangements which were drawn up were, to say the least, remarkable. The revised scheme provided not only for the evacuation of schoolchildren, mothers and babies from the cities, but also for the relocation of Government Departments to what were termed 'neutral areas.' Two schemes were prepared - 'A' making use of terminal railway stations with 'B' as a fall back in the event of the stations not being available. In the interests of security, no indication was to be given in advance of an emergency as to which particular Departments were to be billeted in an area. In addition, strict instructions were issued to the effect that *'no Department should attempt to investigate the billeting position locally or establish contact with local authorities.'*[2] Secrecy was highly regarded. The various Committees dealing with the question of evacuation generally met in private session and most of the associated correspondence at the time was endorsed 'Secret'.

In early 1939 it was decided that, in the event of an emergency situation, the Cabinet Office should be relocated at Hindlop Hall, Worcester with Parliament itself at Stratford on Avon.[3] Other proposals included the transfer of the BBC's main centre to a country house in Worcester, the relocation of the National Film Library's two million feet of priceless film archives to Sussex, and the storage of some of the National Gallery treasures in a cave at a disused quarry in North Wales. In addition, following consultation with the Treasury, the Bank of England was making plans to relocate its various operations and it was also decided to evacuate the Bankers' Clearing House from Post Office Court, London.

In March of that year Germany annexed Czechoslovakia and the British and French Governments opened negotiations with Russia with a view to forming a peace bloc against the Nazi threat. These talks failed and on 23rd August Germany and Russia signed a Nazi-Soviet pact. In the meantime the eyes of the German leaders had began to wander across the Polish border, the subsequent invasion of that country occurring on 1st September.

By this period many Britons, feeling that war was imminent, began to leave for areas of safety, some even venturing abroad if they were in a position to afford it. In addition, for the first time in history, Members of Parliament along with thousands of school teachers and others, all enjoying their summer break, were recalled by means of special BBC radio broadcasts. On the move also were some of the large companies, including Prudential Assurance which sent 450 employees to Torquay, and on 26th August two special trains containing bank officials left London for Trentham in North Staffordshire. The exodus had begun!

NOTES
1. W.S.Churchill Invasion by Air June 1936. Reprinted for the War Cabinet 16th June 1940.
2. PRO File CAB21/604.Hollis to Macgregor 22nd June 1939.
3. PRO Files CAB21/603-6

Chapter 2
Counter Plans

*'It is most inconsiderate of Hitler to make all this fuss,
just at the beginning of the football season!'*
Observer in Evening Sentinel, 26th August 1939

Britain's banking is conducted by means of a highly developed, closely co-ordinated system, the strength and stability of which is reflected in the public confidence by which it is supported. In wartime, more than ever, it is essential that the system does not falter and that confidence is maintained.

The Nazi annexations of Austria and Czechoslovakia made the period from 1938 one of urgent preparation from the Banks' point of view, just as it did in Britain generally. Even before war broke out, full control of the volume of bank deposits with direct intervention on the international exchange for sterling rested with the Government, acting through the Bank of England. Quite apart from this, the Banks were busily engaged with their own measures of protection and safeguard whilst at the same time providing valuable technical advice to the Government.

In London, the Bankers' Clearing House at Post Office Court was the nerve centre through which cheques passed to and from every part of the country. Representatives of member Banks attended at the premises daily, bringing cheques paid in by customers. The cheques were then listed and exchanged in total between the Banks, final balances only being paid over by transfers on Bank of England accounts, wherever due, at the end of the day. Divided into sections for Town, Metropolitan and Country clearings, the premises handled a very large volume of work. In 1938 alone, a daily average of a million cheques passed through its machinery, representing approximately £130 million pounds.[1] It was obvious that the clearing operation could not remain in so vulnerable a location. As a consequence, on 18th August 1938 at a meeting held at the premises, it was resolved to form a special Sub-Committee to consider Emergency Clearings.

The Sub-Committee was chaired by Ernest Sykes, the Secretary General of the Committee of London Clearing Bankers, and consisted of Messrs R.H.Cutting (National Provincial); H.J.Hutchens (Lloyds); T.Mabey (Midland); and H.A.Maggs (Westminster). Setting about its task without delay, the Sub-Committee's interim report was presented on 5th September to a meeting of the Clearing Banks' Chief Accountants and other experts, when it was agreed that a single Central Clearing should be established outside London (i.e. the operation was to be relocated as one unit to handle all clearings - Town, Metropolitan and Country). It was also agreed to consult postal and other appropriate authorities regarding possible sites for relocation. The minutes of the meeting, endorsed 'strictly confidential', also recommended the use of Recordak photographic machines at the proposed Central Clearing House and that enquiries should be made to ensure that sufficient stocks were available.

All the recommendations were subsequently accepted and endorsed by the Clearing Banks' Chief Executive Officers on 13th October. Those present on that occasion were A.W.Tuke (Barclays); C.R.Malcolm (Coutts & Co); E.R.Bardsley (District); B.Currie (Glyn, Mills & Co); R.A.Wilson (Lloyds); R.V.Buxton (Martins); H.A.Astbury (Midland); S.Archer (National); R.N.Smith (National Provincial); C.Lidbury (Westminster); & C.H.Scott (Williams Deacon's).[2]

Basically, the site chosen for relocation had to satisfy two conditions. Firstly, it had to be considered to be in a 'safe area' by the Treasury. Secondly, the site had to be capable of being fully serviced by the postal and railway authorities which, in turn, had to be able to guarantee that the 7,000 or so letters received daily could be transported and delivered with 'reasonable expedition'.[3]

The elaborate preparations that resulted in the successful evacuation of the Bankers' Clearing House were generally based on the foresight of officials and the decision to relocate was not taken lightly. In 1938-39, no-one could accurately predict the likely weight of air attack to be expected, or forecast what fresh demands would be placed upon the banking system in war-time conditions. Little guidance could be gleaned from the experience of the First World War when aircraft were at an early stage of development and, in any event, records of that period were scattered and incomplete. In addition, it was difficult to predict how many trained Bank staff would be retained when large numbers were called to the colours. However, by 17th March 1939 the Treasury indicated that the Banks, including the Bank of England and the Clearing House were 'working well together' and 'well forward with their arrangements'.[4]

The records appertaining to the evacuation of Government Departments and businesses are, as already stated, incomplete, but a secret schedule indicating those areas considered to be suitable for relocation, has survived.[5] Referred to as 'neutral areas' it is not specific about locations but merely lists certain Shire Counties which are then sub-divided into local authority districts.

To what extent regard was had to this document by Treasury and Bank officials in relation to the evacuation of the clearing operation from London is uncertain. In any event, the existence of Trentham Gardens in North Staffordshire was drawn to the attention of the special Sub-Committee early in its deliberations, as the site was considered to satisfy requirements. In February 1939 a delegation was dispatched to report on the site, the former home of the Duke & Duchess of Sutherland, situated about 3 miles south of Stoke-on-Trent.[6] As it happens, Staffordshire does appear on the secret list of the so called 'neutral areas'. Also indicated are the former Stoke-on-Trent City and Newcastle-under-Lyme Borough areas, these being the local authorities nearest to the Trentham Estate at that time.

As to what criteria were applied in determining what was a 'safe' or 'neutral' area is not evident. For example, had those responsible checked thoroughly into the matter, they would have ascertained that North Staffordshire was, in fact, one of those few areas outside London which had suffered bomb damage during the First World War! One such occasion was on 27th November 1916 when a German Zeppelin flew over the area and dropped bombs on Tunstall, Chatterley, Goldendale and Sideway before 'lumbering off like a huge airborne whale in the direction of Derby'.[7] In any event, Trentham Gardens, or more particularly its vast ballroom, was approved for relocation of the clearing operation and terms agreed including a rental of £3,500 per annum for the period 'while the premises are occupied as a result of war'.[8]

In the meantime, additional equipment for the move was placed on order, mainly with firms in London's East End. Billeting and catering arrangements were also put in hand and the Clearing House staff advised to prepare for evacuation to North Staffordshire, the transfer operation being placed under the personal supervision of Mr R.F.Chatham, the Clearing Banks' Chief Inspector.[9]

NOTES
1. J Wadsworth 'Counter Defensive' Hodder & Stoughton p14
2. Minutes of meeting (Clearing House Records)
3. F.W.Hindmarsh 'The Central Clearing House' in The Banker November 1945 p66
4. PRO File CAB21/1060 Rae to Sir Edward Bridges 17th March 1939
5. PRO File CAB21/603-6 The list which has survived relates to a meeting of the Civil Defence Sub-Committee held on 24th October1940. However, it is evident that this, or a forerunner, had been in existence in 1938.
6. F.W.Hindmarsh op.cit p67
7. Ex information from the late Mrs A.E.Bebbington. Reference to bombing of the period is also to be found in the records of the former North Staffs Railway Co - see Evening Sentinel 21st January 1991
8. The lease, which appears not to have survived, was dated 16th August 1939 and is referred to in a letter from the Acting Secretary of the Bankers' Clearing House to Messrs Taylor & Humbert dated 6th June 1945 (the latter being agents for the Trentham Estate). Details of the rental sum were kindly supplied by the Curator of the Bank of England
9. R.F.Chatham became a distinguished lawn tennis umpire and was one time Hon.Secretary of the Lawn Tennis Umpires Association of Great Britain. He officiated in many major tournaments including the gentlemen's singles final between Laver & McKinley in 1961.

The Ballroom Bank; **Central** Clearing House, Trentham, 1939. *APACS*

Chapter 3
The Central Clearing House, Trentham

'The day war broke out my missus said to me -
"It's up to you....you've got to stop it."
I said "stop what?" She said "the war!"

Robb Wilton

What might be termed 'Operation E' took place on Saturday 26th August 1939 when over 900 members of the Clearing House staff left Broad Street station, London in 2 special trains bound for Trentham, and for what was to be their war-time quarters. Machinery and equipment had been sent on by road in advance and, in fact, the media reported large numbers of convoys of lorries leaving the capital as the evacuation generally gathered momentum.[1]

Even with war imminent there was, according to Lady Betty Bryan, a 'holiday atmosphere' surrounding the evacuation. She and her colleagues had been sent home early on the previous day to prepare for the move, but there was a general belief that hostilities would be over by Christmas. As a consequence, life continued with an air of unreal normality. Another former member of the Clearing House staff, Mrs L.R.Pennell, recalls that she spent the day assisting her parents to pick plums before casually proceeding to the railway station for the evacuation. She confirms the leisurely and carefree atmosphere and also recollects the amount of sports gear in evidence among her colleagues' luggage!

In a contemporary magazine article another former member of staff wrote of the evening evacuation journey north and the arrival at Trentham when a voice from the darkness ordered - 'Keep your seats please!' All the passengers, or so it seemed. hung out of the carriage windows straining their eyes and starring into the darkness. Not a sign of habitation could be observed and the only indication of life was at the far end of the train from where muffled voices could be heard and a few dim lanterns could be seen waving. After more lamp waving the locomotive was transferred from the front of the carriages to the rear, following which the whole train proceeded slowly down the branch line to Trentham Park station. Within a few minutes it arrived at its final destination where all passengers were requested to disembark. It was now 12.30am and the weary travellers left the station to find a convoy of buses waiting which they were requested to board. As each became full the vehicles moved off into the darkness, each with an evacuation officer on board, to their destinations. After a short journey the

November 1940.
Chief Inspector R F Chatham, who masterminded the transfer from London to Trentham.

Mrs M Royals

Sunday 28 August 1939; Bank staff, arriving at Trentham for the first time, prepare to move in to establish Central Clearing House for the duration of the war.   *E W Forster*

vehicle would frequently halt. The evacuation officer would then alight, knock on the door of a property and a number of passengers would be allocated accommodation which had previously been reserved with the owner. Following this repetitive procedure, it was well into the early hours of Sunday morning before the last of the passengers arrived at their billets. In fact, at one or two properties, admittance was refused in view of the late hour!

Nevertheless, regardless of the time, the majority of travellers were welcomed and everything possible done to make them comfortable.[2] In effect, there was no shortage of accommodation following earlier appeals in the local newspapers. Many in the south of the city responded and the Evening Sentinel subsequently reported that the appeals had been 'successful'.[3] For those families willing to accommodate bank officials, the terms were 21 shillings per person per week.

All members of staff were instructed to report to Trentham Gardens on the Sunday morning, a period when prayers for peace were being offered at churches throughout North Staffordshire.[4] Despite a tiring journey and with little sleep, the majority arrived early and were pleasantly surprised at the spaciousness and attractiveness of the 800 acre site. Walking from the entrance along the tree lined estate road, the famous ballroom with its innumerable French windows came into view but they were also delighted to see, *'in perfect weather conditions,'* the magnificent gardens, lake and woodlands. Soon the men, *'some in short sleeves, others in plus fours and city clothes'* were *'vigorously engaged'* unloading and moving furniture and office equipment to their required positions. Other items of equipment and machinery, having arrived in advance and stored in the stables, were unpacked and transferred to the ballroom, whilst electricians were busily engaged in the installation of additional lighting and services. All this frantic activity was witnessed by a number of members of the public, one of whom was heard to express doubt that the ballroom would be ready for its intended use in 24 hours, but it was![5] Recalling that Sunday morning and all the activity, Mrs L R Pennell was most impressed by the organisation and planning which had obviously occurred.

However, lack of floor space was only one of many problems which had to be solved quickly. The new Central Clearing House or CCH, as it was to be known, required 40,000 sq.ft. of floor space and there was a significant shortfall in this. Fortunately, from 1937, officials had been compiling statistics of the number of clearings by each Bank and space was allocated at Trentham in proportion to those figures. As a consequence, Midland, Westminster and Barclays were assigned to the floor of the ballroom; Lloyds and National Provincial were to share the gallery with Glyn, Coutts, District and National; an area almost above the kitchen was to house a section of the Bank of England with Williams occupying the stage. Martins were to conduct their business from a small outbuilding.[6]

For those Banks whose staff had arrived earlier (for example, those who had been recalled from nearby North Wales holiday resorts) the situation was advantageous as they had already been able to gain some semblance of order within their allocated areas. This was accomplished by the early 'requisitioning' of cupboards etc. Others were less fortunate in having to store documents and stationery etc under tables and in odd corners.[7]

On the following morning, the day on which the Evening Sentinel announced the closure of Trentham Gardens ballroom and restaurant until further notice,[8] the new Central Clearing House was operational. Not surprisingly, however, having transferred clearing operations from London, there were initial problems. Nevertheless, within an amazingly short period the work was running smoothly.[9] To some extent, the installation of microphotographic apparatus greatly assisted in this, enabling each cheque to be photographed, providing a far swifter and more complete form of record. Eventually, as staff became more familiar with the equipment, 4,000 cheques per hour could be dealt with on each machine and for one Bank section alone, 30 machines were in use.[10] Thus, in the event of loss of cheques arising from enemy action, prints could be made and forwarded to the paying Banker. This system was relied upon extensively when the Channel Islands were occupied.

How essential it was to sustain the flow of work may be appreciated when it is realised that each day's duties had to be completed between the morning inward mail and the evening outward post. No relief could be obtained by a system of shift working and a reserve bank of machines was created to assist in the event of an emergency situation. To aid operations the Paymaster General, Inland Revenue and the General Post Office established offices at Trentham. In addition, the Bank of England's Dividend Accounts and part of its Dividend Pay & Loans offices were established at nearby Barlaston Hall. To further facilitate the new arrangements at Trentham, Burroughs Ltd established a comptometer maintenance workshop in the former stable block, and also a training school at a house in the grounds.

Much credit for the swift initial organisation and ultimate success of the Trentham CCH was attributable to its first Comptroller, Percival Stephen Quick. To him fell the enormous responsibility of translating a *'hypothetical scheme into a successful institution'*. This he accomplished as a result of his vision and determination, combined with other qualities such as untiring energy and enthusiasm which became apparent to all with whom he came into contact. Born in Great Yarmouth, Quick was a great motivator and had experienced a distinguished banking career, commencing in 1904 with the London & South West Bank. His services had been loaned to overseas Banks, including Gibraltar and South Africa, and at the time of his appointment as Comptroller of the CCH he was a high ranking official with Barclays.[11] Sir Arthur Bryan recalled that Mr Quick was always friendly, correct and immaculately dressed. He commanded respect but was somewhat irreverently referred to as 'God' by some of the junior members of the staff.

The Newcastle Times reported on the transfer of the Bank officials to their new headquarters at Trentham and that they were lodging with 'large numbers of people in the Potteries.'[12] According to the newspaper they were expected to stay *'for at least six months, whether war breaks out or not.'*

By the time war was declared a few days later, the CCH at Trentham was fully operational. It was, without doubt, a masterpiece of organisation and forward planning.

NOTES
1. Newcastle Times 1st September 1939
2. Anon. 'At Trentham' in 'The Old Lady' June 1940 pp97-98
3. Evening Sentinel 28th September 1939
4. Ibid
5. Anon. op.cit p98 and The Outcast Vol I p6
6. F.W.Hindmarsh op.cit p68
7. Anon. op.cit p98
8. Evening Sentinel 28th August 1939
9. Anon. op.cit p99
10. J Wadsworth op.cit p23
11. The Outcast Vol II p126
12. Newcastle Times op.cit

Post Office and Paymaster General's Section, situated in the foyer.   *Stoke on Trent City Museum*

Trentham Central Clearing House, 23 November 1940. Chief Inspector R F Chatham, left, and H C T Wiltshire. Note the tape on the windows, a precaution against flying glass in the event of bomb blast.   *Courtesy of Mrs M Royals*

First Aid & Rescue Services, comprising staff of all banks.
Mrs L Pennell

First Aid & Rescue Team.
Mrs L Pennell

Chapter 4
The Outcasts

'Hundreds each morning I behold
Into Trentham stalking,
Some are walking to reduce,
But most reduced to walking.'

A.Skilbeck. 'The Outcast' November 1941

Whilst being given brief details of their destination prior to evacuation, little did the members of the Bank fraternity (or 'Outcasts' as they were to call themselves) realise that there would be a language problem on their arrival in North Staffordshire. At that time there were, to my knowledge, no Potteries dialect or phrase books available such as the classic 'Arfur Tow Crate in Staffy Cher' so that initially they had to rely on the friendly natives for translation! For example, called destinations by conductors on bus services serving Trentham would, on occasion, result in a nil response or blank looks from the queue of waiting 'foreigners' as they had no idea where the vehicle was heading. Being war-time, of course, the buses bore no destination signs. But how were they to know that a bellowed "ANLYONLY!" from the conductor meant 'Hanley' or 'Hanley only'? Sir Arthur Bryan also recalls an occasion in the CCH canteen at Trentham when, as a junior member of staff, he requested details of the choice of main course available for lunch. The canteen assistant indicated that it was beef or alternatively, 'silv'rayke' (silver hake!). In turn, Sir Arthur replied that he would have the fish, to which a southerner standing immediately behind promptly enquired - *'how did you know it was fish?'* BBC Radio Stoke's popular presenter Bill Humphreys, a junior employee of Lloyds at the time, confirms the language problem and also that local expressions such as *'ever likely'* reduced the southerners to hysterics. Further, comments on the weather such as *'it's a rayl pay seouper ight theere, duck'* (it's very foggy out there - 'duck' being a local form of endearment, such as dear) did nothing to ease the situation. Not to be left out, the Evening Sentinel newspaper at the time joked of a conversation between a Potteries lad and a Cockney:
The Cockney - *'I think it's going to rine'*
'Dust?' queried the Potteries lad.
'No - rine!' replied the Cockney. [1]

Prior to arrival, the evacuation destination of Trentham in North Staffordshire was of little or no significance to the southerners. Generally, the place name meant nothing to them, but neither did other destinations north of Enfield Chase. For many it was as if life north of the capital did not exist. However, for a minority, it conjured up associations with the Black Country, people in clogs, flat caps and shawls who survived on a diet of tripe and black puddings, whose only interests were pigeons and whippets - an impression of the area still held by many southerners! Nevertheless, North Staffordshire and its people made favourable impressions on the new arrivals. With few exceptions, the Banking staff were most impressed by the warmth of welcome from the locals and, in particular, from those with whom they were billeted. Lady Bryan, for her part, spoke of the relationship with the Potteries folk as being 'harmonious to the extreme.' Many of the southerners were also impressed by the modern shopping facilities and, on visiting Hanley, were surprised to find large stores such as Huntbach's, Lewis's, Bratt & Dyke etc which they considered to be equal to any in London's West End.[2] Others came to appreciate the beautiful Staffordshire countryside, sentiments which they have retained. Those who found themselves in rural billets such as Hanchurch considered themselves to be particularly fortunate after living and/or working in the busy capital.

Fortunately, many of the southerners' impressions of the area were recorded. In February 1940 The Outcast magazine was launched to 'chronicle and entertain' those from the City of London who, by the exigency of war 'found themselves in strange surroundings to carry on a vital national service'.[3] The magazine was published regularly, initially under the joint editorship of Percy Woodruff and John Chater and featured news and events relating to the Central Clearing House whilst at the same time attempting to entertain with varied contributions from staff. Subsequently, it was to provide a valuable service in providing news of former

CCH, Trentham.   *APACS*

colleagues who had been called to the colours. Rarely was reference made to the official work of the establishment! Printed locally by C H Vyse Ltd., the magazine continued to be published until 1943 and, fortunately, copies have survived.

Amongst other things, the first edition featured R.B.Day's poem *'Hiabanking'* (with apologies to Longfellow's 'Hiawatha') in which he gave his impressions of the arrival at Trentham:

> *'You shall hear how up at Trentham*
> *In the Potteries of Stafford*
> *There arrived one night so dismal*
> *In two trains all hot and smoky*
> *Teeming crowds of untamed Bank clerks*
> *Male and female all assorted*
> *Each complete with case and toothbrush*
> *And with things here not reported*
> *How they bunged them,*
> *Stuffed them, rammed them*
> *Into buses cold and cheerless*
> *And by ways so slow and bumpy*
> *Took them for that painful night ride*
> *To the wigwams of Trent Valers*
> *To the parts of distant Westlands*
> *Back again and round the houses*
> *Even to the heights of Longton ....*
>
> *Of the wondrous days that followed*
> *In the ballroom and its precincts*
> *Where machines and men were mingled*
> *Into one complete confusion*
> *And from post bags old and hoary*
> *Poured forth letters in abundance*
> *Each one full of new surprises*
> *Cheques in millions and all sizes.*[4]

In contrast, Marguerite Carter waxed lyrical about the Trentham site in her item
To Stand and Stare:
'The city streets and our suburban gardens exchanged
for wide vistas and far horizons. The country!
(although probably most of us have dreamed more of
a cottage than a ballroom).

Now we have a chance (unimpeded by chimney pots)
of learning which star it is that hangs poised
like a Christmas fairy above that far pine; of hearing
the hoot of the little owl as he goes hunting
near the darkling woods; and of learning something of
the variety of trees that go marching in such
beauty across the Park. [5]

On the other hand, Dorothy M. Horton in her 'A Study in Contrasts' compared the former London premises with the new venue at Trentham:

> *'For the sombre dignity of a room in which the*
> *green shaded table lamps shed dim reflections*
> *on mahogany and brass and from which one heard only*
> *an obligato of the distant rumble of traffic, we were*
> *to exchange the spaciousness of a modern ballroom foyer,*
> *sunshine streaming gaily in on scarlet tables and on*
> *a counter which obstinately refused to wear anything*
> *but the jaunty air of a cocktail bar...*
> *This then was to be the mise-en-scene of our 'office'.*[6]

There was, however, one North Staffordshire characteristic which did not impress the southerners, this being the local bus services. In this respect, John Summers wrote of his frustrations in 'They Go Past the Gates' - bus queue reflections:

> *'How frequently do we curse having to wait for*
> *buses to take us home in the evenings from the*
> *CCH and consign all bus companies, their directors*
> *and staff to the region noted for intense heat.'* [7]

In similar vein, another colleague observed:

> *'A Potteries bus is a thing that starts from*
> *the Gardens Gate as you are emerging from*
> *the ballroom vestibule.'* [8]

Local bus services, or rather their inadequacy, were the subject of much debate at the time, the whole question eventually being raised in the House of Commons.[9] Subsequently, a local Police Commander was heard to comment in Churchillian tones - 'Never have so many waited so long for so few!'[10]

Many of the CCH staff solved the problem of transport by hiring cycles from local specialist dealers such as Whittakers in London Road, Stoke. In fact, as it became apparent that they were to remain at Trentham for a lengthy period, the cycles were purchased. Mrs L.R.Pennell recalled how pleasant it was to cycle to work instead of the daily train journeys into London to which she was accustomed. Others chose to walk into Trentham, dependent on their preference, or merely because their billets were in close proximity to the CCH.

District Bank staff at Trentham.   *Mrs L Pennell*

Barclay's staff at Trentham CCH, including a young Arthur Bryan, fourth from left.
Sir Arthur Bryan

September 1941. CCH Staff at Trentham Gardens Pool, on the far side of the lake.
Lady Bryan collection

The swimming pool, Trentham, c1938

The restaurant in 1942, (now the Roman Bar.) This also provided the venue for the Siren Theatre.
Stoke on Trent City Museum

Trentham CCH Fire Squad.
Left to right;
J Forrest, J Emery, W R Collins,
B H Bennett (Comptroller),
W Attewell, P R Barnard,
L de T Stewart, S H Farnell.

Female staff working in the ballroom, obviously under chilly conditions - the majority are wearing their coats! *Stoke on Trent City Museum*

1942. Catering, portering and domestic staff with senior officials gathered in front of the yew trees by the Italian gardens.   *Mrs M Royals*

The Barclay's contingent of the Trentham CCH
Fire Watching team prepared for action.
Sir Arthur Bryan

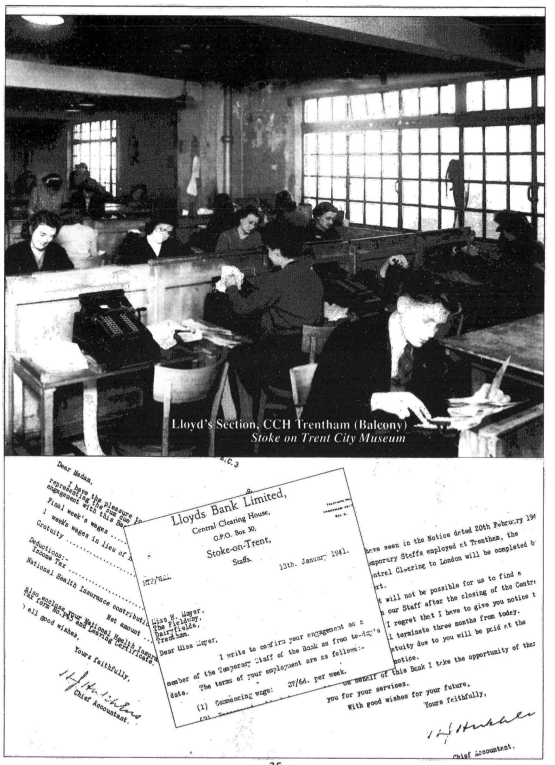

Lloyd's Section, CCH Trentham (Balcony)
Stoke on Trent City Museum

Dear Madam,

I have the pleasure to
representing the sum due to
engagement with this Ba...

Final week's wages ....

1 weeks wages in lieu of ...

Gratuity ....

Deductions:-
Income Tax ....

National Health Insurance contributi...

Also enclose your National Health Insura...
Tax form No.P45 and leaving Certificate.

all good wishes,

Yours faithfully,

Chief Accountant.

Lloyds Bank Limited,

Central Clearing House,
G.P.O. Box 30,
Stoke-on-Trent,
Staffs.

RTP/WLL.

13th. January 1941.

Miss M. Mayer,
The Fieldway,
Dairyfields,
Trentham.

Dear Miss Mayer,

I write to confirm your engagement as a
member of the Temporary Staff of the Bank as from to-day's
date. The terms of your employment are as follows:-

(1) Commencing wage: 27/6d. per week.
(2) ...

...have seen in the Notice dated 20th February 194...

...mporary Staffs employed at Trentham, the
...entral Clearing to London will be completed b...
...xt.

...t will not be possible for us to find a
...n our Staff after the closing of the Centr...
...I regret that I have to give you notice t...
...l terminate three months from today.
...etuity due to you will be paid at the
...notice.

...on behalf of this Bank I take the opportunity of than...
you for your services.

With good wishes for your future,

Yours faithfully,

Chief Accountant.

National Provincial Staff seen against the background of the Orangery in the gardens.   *Mrs M Royals*

Three female members of the National Provincial staff with a member of the armed forces at Trentham Gardens swimming baths. Second from left is Mrs J Butler, who supplied the photograph.

Festive Christmas decorations festoon the gallery above the ballroom.. District Bank staff can be seen in the foreground and National Provincial employees to the rear.   *Mrs L Pennell*

Williams Deacons Bank holding centre stage at Trentham Gardens. *Mrs J Smith*

As the 'Outcasts' settled in at Trentham and became more familiar with their work and new routines, opportunities for leisure and recreation arose. One of the first organised social activities was dancing to gramophone records in the sculpture gallery or, alternatively, the Orangery Restaurant (now known as the Roman Bar). Referred to as 'Bob Hops' one member of staff observed that they took place *on a floor never intended for such purpose as it would have been in the more sophisticated atmosphere of London.* Nevertheless, the events were 'well attended' and 'thoroughly enjoyed'.[11] Another early innovation was the 'House Cinema' which also took place in the sculpture gallery. These were organised in conjunction with Kodak Ltd under whose 'expert direction' silent films were shown to the staff. Coincidentally, one of the first films to be shown at Trentham was Charlie Chaplin's aptly titled 'The Bank'.[12]

For those of the CCH staff who were of a sporting disposition, generous concessions were offered by both Trentham and Trentham Park Golf Clubs. In addition, they soon had unrestricted use of certain local football, hockey, netball, keep fit, cricket and swimming facilities, with the Banks' London Clubs providing their Trentham colleagues with some useful secondhand sports gear.[13] A ladies keep fit class was soon established and it is recorded that the first session in the restaurant was attended by 30 girls 'clad in neat white blouses and black knickers' which, no doubt, was responsible for a rise in blood pressure among the male members of staff![14] Within a short time, other pursuits included squash, athletics, rounders, table tennis and darts and, to co-ordinate all such activities, a Sports Club was formed. The CCH Comptroller, Percival Quick, served as its first President. Members' ties could be purchased for 3s.6d, the design consisting of *a narrow white stripe on a navy background dotted with the City of London arms, surrounded by the Staffordshire Knot.* [15]

Further recreation or leisure could be obtained at break times, or after working hours, at the nearby Monica Cafe. These premises - now 'The Poachers Cottage' - were a favourite haunt of the CCH staff and here, under the management of Mrs Shenton, many delicious meals were taken and special events such as birthdays celebrated. Marguerite Cotton writing in The Outcast magazine cited the Monica Cafe as *an interesting place for students of human nature - within it one can watch the budding (or disbudding!) of romances and the flowering of friendships. One can enter with turmoil in the soul after a particularly hectic day and proceed to 'run' the war, reorganise the Cabinet or one's department to one's content, and depart refreshed in body, mind and spirit!* [16] Coffee breaks were taken here but more generally at a hut on the banks of the Trent within the Trentham Gardens complex. Birthdays were also celebrated at the bar in the Orangery Restaurant, this also serving as the venue for thirst quenching after rehearsals for shows.

On the cultural side, a Drama Club under the chairmanship of C F Fillmore was formed. Its first production, a twenty two scene revue ('& Sharp's the Action') brought praise from the locals, including members of Shelton Repertory Theatre, a well respected group of amateur theatricals, whose premises at Beresford Street, Shelton were used for the lively show. The same production was later used to entertain troops at Hartshill and Stone. Subsequently, contact was to be firmly established with the Shelton company following a visit to their production of J.M. Barrie's comedy 'Dear Brutus' which the southerners found 'much to their liking'.[17] This soon resulted in a production by the Outcasts' Drama Group of Ivor Novello's comedy 'Fresh Fields' under the direction of Leonard Crainford. This ran for six nights, commencing on 15th April 1940. Over two hundred troops from Stone, Hartshill and Keele Hall attended the dress rehearsal and the programme, like that for similar 'Outcast' productions of the period, was endorsed that *'in the event of an air raid warning...the show will continue!'* Other initial cultural pursuits included the formation of a Literary Section, a branch of the local library service in the foyer, an orchestra under Maurice Kettle and a musical society.

For those members of staff who were suffering from minor ailments, a Chemist's shop operated in the foyer of the ballroom, tucked partly beneath the staircase in what today accommodates the reception area. On the other hand, for those suffering from nostalgia or needing to return to London to visit their families, monthly travel vouchers were dispensed.

The attitude towards return journeys by some members of staff is no better described than in Alice Easton's poem:

> *'It's not the going home I mind,*
> *It's the coming back again!*
> *What's five hours journey now to me*
> *Who travel oft by train?*
> *But one five hours I'd gladly do*
> *And never mind the strain.*
> *It's the trek from home to Trentham*
> *That goes against the grain!*
>
> *One day there'll be rejoicing,*
> *And loud the glad refrain:*
> *'We're going home! We're going home!*
> *We won't be back again!'*
>
> *But till that glorious day appears*
> *I'll travel oft by train,*
> *Five hours each way a-journeying,*
> *Nor think it done in vain.*
>
> *For be the journey ne'er so dull,*

39

The country ne'er so plain,
The company makes up for all
Once I'm at home again.
For home and friends and family
I'll gladly take the train,
It's not the going home I mind,
It's the coming back again.' [18]

An early edition of The Outcast magazine also observed that *'a medical certificate is a document, particularly indigenous to North Staffordshire, which testifies that the bearer is suffering from nostalgia.'* [19]

In the meantime, the beautiful Autumn weather had drawn to a close, heralding the arrival of shorter, darker, winter days. As the southerners approached their first Christmas in North Staffordshire, it became apparent that the lighting in the CCH was totally inadequate, comprising nothing more than 60w bulbs. Requests to 'lighten our darkness' eventually resulted in these being replaced with 100w which much improved the situation. [20]

When the Christmas of 1939 did arrive it was most unusual to say the least. Falling as it did in the so called 'phoney war' it was a strange period of quiet, bewilderment and rumour. The anticipated bombing of London at the outset of war had not materialised, neither had any apparent attempt at invasion. Moreover, the mass evacuation to 'safe' areas meant that thousands were eating Christmas meals in other people's homes. Any carol singers were obliged to ensure that their lanterns did not shine too conspicuously, and were also prohibited from ringing bells to avoid any confusion with air raid warnings. In addition, many churches throughout the country cancelled midnight services because of the difficulty of blacking out large stained glass windows.

Yet in North Staffordshire, the Evening Sentinel in a pre-Christmas edition reported that traders and postal and rail officials were in agreement that *'the war had not dampened the Christmas spirit'*, with a prediction of the *'heaviest Christmas period on record for both passengers and parcels traffic'*. For the first five days of Christmas week, cards and letter post were reported as being 'up by 430,000' [21]

Subsequently however, to the threat of more males being called up for military service, North Staffordshire, in common with the rest of the country, chose to celebrate New Year with unaccustomed quiet. [22] Although some churches held midnight services and a few dance halls opened, thoughts of what 1940 might bring tended to depress any celebrations that were held.

The Evening Sentinel heralded the New Year with a series of morale boosting messages from civic and church leaders whose dominant theme was '*the resolute determination of all sections of the community to prosecute the war to a victorious issue and thereby to secure a conclusive and lasting peace.*' Also in that same issue was a surprise report from Reuters claiming that Hitler had contracted cancer, as a result of which his life expectancy was only 18 months![23] Irrespective of whether this was fact, or merely a propaganda ploy, the Bank staff at Trentham were busily engaged in their own defence measures.

Among other things, the CCH boasted its own fire fighting squad comprising 46 personnel complete with a Beresford motor pump, a gas detector squad of 10 personnel, a car squad of 20 for conveying serious casualties to hospital and a 250 strong ARP squad - all volunteers! Other members of staff joined local units of the Auxiliary Fire Service, Special Constables and Local Defence Volunteers - the LDV cynically referred to by some as 'Look, duck & vanish!' (later the Home Guard). All CCH units drilled regularly to ensure that they were not only capable of dealing with an emergency situation but also of handling the various items of specialist apparatus involved.[24] Bill Humphreys, in particular, recalled wrestling with the powerful fire hoses and also of being on night fire watching duty, on top of the ballroom.

The CCH also possessed a 'great army of knitters' whose work was co-ordinated by the organisers of a Knitting & Comforts Fund, the proceeds of which ensured the provision of parcels of 'goodies' for those colleagues who were on active service. In addition, the fund enabled cigarettes, coffee etc to be provided when troops were being entertained locally. On occasion, donations were also made to local charity funds such as that of the British Red Cross.[25]

During early 1940 the 'Outcasts' continued to forge links with local organisations and industry. For example, an early visitor to the CCH was John Cook, Curator of the Wedgwood Museum who gave a talk in the sculpture gallery on the pottery industry of North Staffordshire. Subsequently, a large party of the CCH staff visited the Wedgwood factory at Etruria.[26] Coincidentally, a Rambling Club had been formed and with guidance from the local Hanliensians Rambling Club, an outing to Dovedale was arranged. The Hanliensians continued to advise the newly formed club for a while and examples of contemporary ramble itineries include Beresford Dale, the Dove Valley and Three Shires Head. Later in the year, however, this activity had to be temporarily suspended owing to difficulty in hiring private coaches. However, they were later resumed by utilising service buses and splitting into smaller groups.[27] In the Spring a party of CCH staff visited Kibblestone at the personal invitation of Ronald Copeland, the Acting County Scout Commissioner. It is recorded that, at the time of the visit, 'the drive to the hall was looking beautiful with drifts of daffodils and crocuses. Wherever one looked there were flowers.'[28] Outings such as this proved to be immensely popular with the southerners who came to appreciate Staffordshire's beautiful countryside, particularly after working in the contrasting busy capital.

On 14th March 1940 one of the first of many concerts featuring 'Outcast' Maurice Kettle took place at Trentham. The recital, also featuring Stella Wheeler (violin), included works by Schumann, Albeniz, Bach, Corelli and Vivaldi.[29] An official of the Westminster Bank, Kettle was a pianist of repute, and his style and approach was much appreciated by those who attended his concerts. Until such time as he joined the services in 1941, he went on to organise many other concerts in and around the area, on occasion featuring a composition of his own and conducting the orchestra which he had formed with the aid of colleagues from the CCH staff. Another aspect of the entertainment at Trentham was the regular Smoking Concerts in what is now the restaurant. Typical of these was one featuring Kettle with Nancy Hines (two pianos) with accompanying artistes including Brynmor Jones (baritone) and Mary Perry (soprano) which was attended by an audience in excess of 400.[30] Whilst not joining the establishment until 1942, Bill Humphreys nevertheless recalls the Smoking Concerts with much pleasure and comments that they probably would be frowned upon now. But they were extremely popular and an important feature of the entertainment and Bill, like so many other locals, appreciated being exposed to the rich cultural life of the southerners which broadened his musical experience, hitherto confined largely to being a chorister at Blurton Church.

There was more activity on the sporting front and on 11th April 1940 a team of 'Outcasts' played H.G.H. William's XI at the PMT ground near the Trentham Hotel. Mrs Wenger of 'The Priory' officiated at the kick-off and both teams were rather impressed in having Stoke City & England footballer Stanley Matthews (later Sir) as a linesman.[31] The 'Outcasts' possessed a remarkable selection of talent in their ranks, not only in the cultural field but also in sport. For example, when the cricket season commenced, they were able to field two County players - John Marriott (Herts) and Vic Jervis (Essex). Marriott was described at the time as 'one of the foremost bowlers in club cricket' but both players made valuable contributions before being called to the colours.[32]

At the end of April, there was more culture in the form of a concert given by the Outcasts' Musical Society under the baton of Alfred Henry Pinnington, its ambitious programme including part of Coleridge-Taylor's 'Hiawatha's Wedding Feast'.[33] Described as a *'large man of the Sergeant Major variety'*, Pinnington was one of Barclay's senior officials at Trentham. A member of the Royal Choral Society, his name was to become firmly engraved in the cultural history of North Staffordshire.

Meanwhile, across the water in Scandinavia, the Germans had occupied the neutral states of Denmark and Norway following which Allied forces landed on the west coast at Namsos and Andalsnes intending to take the port of Trondheim. Unfortunately, they did not succeed and after a fortnight withdrew. At Narvik in the north, the navy destroyed German ships which had seized the port and an Allied force eventually recaptured the town. This proved to be a solitary success as the Allied troops were subsequently withdrawn due to the dangerous situation which was developing in France and the Low Countries. This, strange as it may seem, was to have significant implications for Trentham.

NOTES
1. Evening Sentinel 18th November 1939
2. The Outcast March 1940 p27
3. Outcast Observer June 1940 Editorial
4. The Outcast Vol I p15
5. Ibid p30
6. Ibid p17
7. The Outcast Vol II p278
8. The Outcast Vol I p81
9. Evening Sentinel 2nd November 1939
10. Ibid 28th February 1942
11. The Outcast Vol I p7
12. Ibid p39
13. Ibid p21
14. Ibid pp49-50
15. Ibid pp51-52
16. The Outcast Vol III p3
17. The Outcast Vol I p29
18. Ibid p63
19. Ibid p81
20. Ibid p17
21. Evening Sentinel 21st December 1939
22. Ibid 31st December 1939
23. Ibid lst January 1940
24. The Outcast Vol I p176
25. Ibid p176
26. Ibid pp71 & 113
27. Ibid pp48 & 127
28. Ibid p86
29. Ibid p70
30. Ibid p115
31. Ibid p89
32. Ibid p91
33. Ibid p116

Chapter 5
The French Camp

*'Nightingales may sing in Berkeley Square,
but there are far more varieties of birds singing in the Gardens'*
Marguerite Carter, Outcast Magazine, Vol II p97

During the Second World War thousands of foreign troops were present in parts of North Staffordshire which had a profound influence on the life of the area. Among the first, in June 1940, were French servicemen at Trentham Park, following the fall of France. However, their arrival was preceded by that of 505 Field Company, Royal Engineers on 17th June under orders to 'stage a camp'.[1]

Whilst the officer in charge may have known the precise reasoning for 505 Company's transfer to Trentham from Knutsford, the rank and file did not. According to Mr C Parker, who served with the unit, he and his colleagues were merely required to erect a large quantity of bell tents in the parkland in 'precise military lines' and to dig long latrine trenches, much to the consternation of neighbouring residents. To aggravate the situation further, some of the tents were erected on part of the adjacent golf course and this, according to Mr Parker, soon led to protests from club officials. Notwithstanding, the reason for the camp soon became apparent with the 'arrival of 4000 Frenchmen'![2] The majority of these comprised survivors of the 13th Foreign Legion half brigade - 13th DBLE (demi Brigade de la Legion Etrangere) and that of a half brigade of the Chasseurs Alpins (Mountain Light Infantry).

Both the 13th DBLE, and the Chasseurs Alpins, had formed part of an allied force sent to Norway on 23rd April 1940 in a strategy designed to prevent much needed Swedish ore reaching Germany. The bulk of this was being exported through the Norwegian ice-free port of Narvik. Both regiments had fought with great effect in Norway, but the imminent collapse of the French army at home resulted in their premature recall. Unfortunately, they arrived at Brest to witness briefly the chaos of the French defeat by the Germans and it was quickly concluded that there was nothing to be gained at that stage by fighting. Consequently, they re-embarked for England with their arms and equipment, arriving at Trentham Park between 19th-21st June, having travelled by train from Barry and various ports on the south coast.

The officer commanding the 13th DBLE was Lt.Colonel Raoul Magrin-Vernerey (later 'Montclar' of the Resistance), a hero of the First World War. Wounded on seventeen

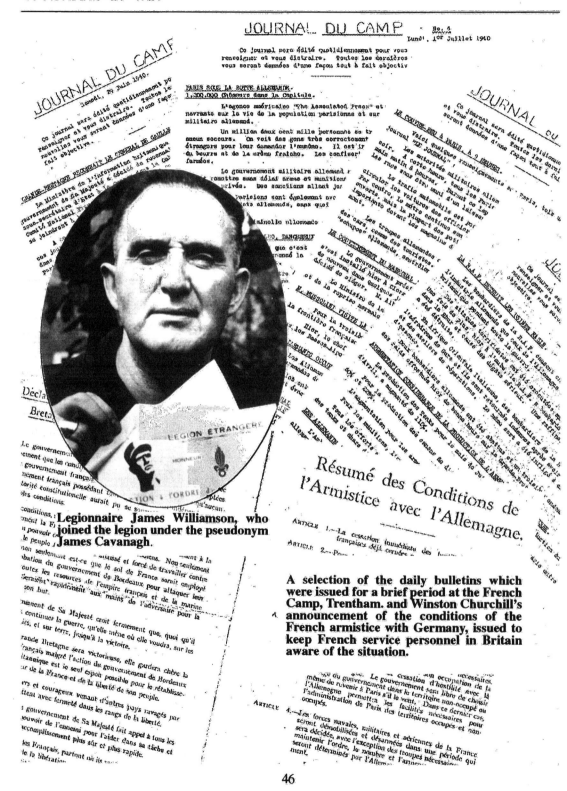

JOURNAL DU CAMP

Legionnaire James Williamson, who joined the legion under the pseudonym James Cavanagh.

A selection of the daily bulletins which were issued for a brief period at the French Camp, Trentham, and Winston Churchill's announcement of the conditions of the French armistice with Germany, issued to keep French service personnel in Britain aware of the situation.

occasions, his career had been primarily with the Legion since 1924. He and two fellow officers (Major Pierre Koenig and Captain Dimitri Amilakvari) had returned to Brest following a reconnaissance expedition of the Liffre forest near Rennes, only to find that their regiment had left for England without them. Escaping in a small boat to Southampton, they met up with a number of legionnaires who had arrived earlier and all were ordered to board a train for Trentham where they arrived on 21st June. On arrival they found the park area already full with other French service personnel including a number of sailors. [3] Also encamped were elements of the Polish Highland Brigade (the Carpathian Chasseurs), this unit consisting of Polish personnel who had earlier fled to France.

As one can imagine, the sheer scale of operation in organising the vast camp at Trentham presented many problems. For example, in addition to the erection of the camp itself, there were also the associated problems of feeding, administering and the control of approximately 5000 foreign troops many of whose adrenalin was flowing having been thrust into the area almost direct from battle. To add to this, some of the new arrivals were in need of replacement clothing, items of kit having been lost during the escape from France. It is recorded that the legionnaires were issued with standard British battle-dress at Trentham, which they wore with the khaki French beret - *'the cherished white kepi having been 'put away' for the time being.'*[4] Some were fortunate in being allocated accommodation immediately on arrival, others were not. Consequently, ex-servicemen's memories of the period are naturally influenced by those particular conditions and events that they experienced at that time.

For example, M.Jean Massoulard (5th half brigade, Chasseurs Alpins) appreciated the warm reception from British officials on his arrival at Trentham Park on the evening of 21st June. He was most impressed by the 'efficiency of British military organisation' and with the tents, cooking apparatus and services provided. Recalling Trentham with *'its vast park, woods and the enormous lake full of fish,'* he felt almost as if he was 'on holiday in the country'. He added, however, that it rained heavily on the night of his arrival![5]

Another correspondent recalled that on arrival, he was *'quartered in a bell tent with eight men, feet inwards towards the centre pole in a star pattern, but on a sloping site.'* By the morning, all had rolled down the slope which resulted in the occupants sleeping *'in a heap at the lower side of the tent!'*[6]

In contrast, Legionnaire James Williamson, one of the 1619 survivors of the 13th DBLE, did not fare so well. Such were the numbers to be provided for that it was days

Brenda Meaney (now Kitching) with
French sailor in Trentham gardens, seated
by the rose trellis on the Rainbow Walk..
Mrs B Kitching

25 August 1940. King George V1 with General de
Gaulle, reviewingFrench troops at Trentham Park.

Newcastle under Lyme 1940.
Members of the French forces, in their distinctive
cloaks.   *Newcastle Borough Museum*

Newcastle under Lyme 1940.
Members of the Polish Highland Brigade
Newcastle Borough Museum

Trentham Park 1940. French officers enjoy a cigarette with a British colleague.　　*Evening Sentinel*

Trentham Park 1940. French sailors hang their washing!　　　*Evening Sentinel*

before he and some of his colleagues were assigned proper accommodation and issued with rations. Initially, they slept 'under the stars' until eventually provided with bell tents. Having joined the legion in 1937 under the pseudonym James Cavanagh, Williamson had fought in the Norway campaign gaining the Croix de Guerre with bronze star and the Barrettes Norvege. However, by a trick of fate, this particular legionnaire was well acquainted with the Trentham estate, having been born in Stoke-on-Trent. Thus, whilst the camp perimeter was ringed with barbed wire and manned by guards, this did not prevent Williamson from undertaking nocturnal visits to friends and relatives. Having said that, however, he did admit to having spent the occasional night wrapped in his cloak in the macabre surroundings of the Sutherland mausoleum, rather than attempt to enter camp in the early hours, having sampled the local brews. In any event, the perimeter fencing was too vast to be fully effective and this, coupled with insufficient numbers on guard patrol, meant that security was not entirely successful. After a while, free access was allowed to those who were authorised or wished to leave the camp temporarily, but those entering were strictly vetted.

Rations generally consisted of potatoes, cabbage and corned beef and these were cooked over wood fires in old style washing boilers or olive oil tins to provide a stew (or North Staffordshire 'lobby'). However, Williamson also supplemented food rations for his colleagues with 'imported' supplies of fish and chips, portions of which were sometimes used to bribe his Sergeant. On other occasions, he recalled, venison was poached from the Park's deer herd.[7]

Meanwhile, the decision by the French government to capitulate to the Germans, rather than fight on, had not been accepted by all Frenchmen. On Tuesday 18th June, the anniversary of the Battle of Waterloo, General Charles de Gaulle broadcast at 10pm his personal refusal to surrender to Germany, together with a rallying call to all Frenchmen for continued resistance. Speaking from the BBC's Studio 4D in London, de Gaulle's voice of revolt rang out, according to J.Gunther, *'like trumpet blasts around the world'*[8] Saying in effect that France had lost a battle, but not the war, he appealed to all Frenchmen to rally to his standard - *'the flame of French resistance cannot go out. It will not go out'.*[9] Thus began the Free French movement.

Not surprisingly, within a short time, a climate of uneasiness began to develop within the French camp at Trentham, the population of which had now increased to 5530.[10] Bewildered by events in France and confused about their status few, if any, were able to grasp a fundamental understanding of the situation. Nothing was initially known of the terms of the armistice and the majority tended to believe that the war was over and that they could return to France. In addition, a number of units had lost their officers and/or NCOs and thus, lacked leadership, which did not help communications. The situation at Trentham Park was also not helped by the fact that the French troops, having recently fought bravely in the Norway campaign with a number having been highly decorated, were being guarded by British troops - their allies. The air of uneasiness resulted in the guards being 'nervous', James Williamson recalled, and if anything happened to be wrong the blame was generally placed on the shoulders of the legionnaires.

The fact that a tense atmosphere was developing had also been observed by George Wigg (later Lord Wigg) when he visited Trentham Park on 24th June. On that occasion he had expressed a view to the camp's British Liaison Officer that *'a dangerous situation was threatening, the French troops being restless, armed and far from friendly'*. However, the latter disagreed. Notwithstanding, Wigg made a detailed report to the War Office.[11] Possibly as a consequence of this, when Wigg visited the camp on a subsequent occasion, he was held at rifle point for half an hour while his papers were checked.[12] Discontent was perhaps more rife among the volatile Spanish legionnaires of the 13th DBLE who, according to D.Porch, 'retained a mind of their own that any amount of Legion discipline seemed powerless to alter'.[13] This finally erupted on 25th June, the day when the armistice between France and Germany became effective, when 29 Spaniards refused to muster as a result of which they were handed over to the British police. This provoked many of the remaining Spaniards into disobeying orders and they too suffered the same fate. This action unfortunately provoked further discontent among those remaining at the camp who felt that the British police had no jurisdiction to deal with the Spanish legionnaires who were, after all, *'yesterday's brothers in combat'*.

On 28th June, the British Government announced its official recognition of General de Gaulle as 'the leader of all Free Frenchmen, wherever they may be, who rally to him in support of the allied cause'[14] and on the following day he made a brief visit to Trentham Park. Having given the troops a choice of repatriation to North Africa, or fighting on with the Free French, de Gaulle subsequently wrote in his memoirs of being able to rally 'a major part of two battalions of the Foreign Legion, about 200 Chasseurs Alpins, two-thirds of a tank company and a few remnants of artillery, engineers, signallers, etc. *'This,'* he added, was *'in spite of the fact that two British Colonels in turn had had the troops paraded in order to tell them literally - "you are perfectly free to serve under General de Gaulle. But it is our duty to point out to you, speaking as man to man, that if you do so decide you will be rebels against your Government"'.*[15] Lt Colonel Magrin-Vernerey decided to join de Gaulle and, in doing so, perhaps influenced some of his men. Those who were not so influenced and who opted for repatriation possibly did so as a result of war weariness or, alternatively, a dose of the so called 'Anglophobia'. This, according to D.Porch, was stimulated by the mass evacuation from Dunkirk which many French regarded as a 'treacherous defection rather than a miraculous escape'.[16] It also resulted from uncomplimentary remarks relating to French martial qualities by certain British civilians living around Trentham Park.[17]

It would be misleading, however, to give a general impression that the French servicemen were unpopular with the residents in North Staffordshire. To begin with, as one might perhaps expect, they were extremely popular with many of the female population of the area. Recalling the period, Mrs Jean Butler states that being young and impressionable, she and some of her colleagues at the Central Clearing House were 'bowled over' by the sight of the 'truly romantic looking lot of soldiers with their jaunty berets, swinging cloaks and swarthy looks - 'Beau Geste' before our very eyes!' Also, local 'talent' would frequently pour from the buses at Trentham hoping for dates with the Frenchmen or merely glimpses of them. The French troops also proved to be popular with locals at the dances which were held at the Pavilion Cafe, Hanford. The Italian proprietor of the premises, Mario Togneni. was himself extremely popular with residents, being particularly noted for his excellent ice cream. When he, together with a number of other highly respected residents of foreign extraction, was interned for a temporary period as a result of a Government decision to detain all 'aliens',[18] the measure proved to be unpopular with the indigenous population. Many of the so called 'aliens' from North Staffordshire were interned at a camp at Prees Heath, near Market Drayton which was operative only for a short period. This particular legislation, however, caused much distress and suffering to many similar people across Britain, a large number being from well established business families whose loyalties were entirely with this country.

Another popular venue with the French, particularly the officers, was the tea rooms at 'West View', Ash Green. Mrs I Moss recalls the visits by the French and other service personnel who frequently patronised the premises which were then owned by her mother, Mrs P Moreton. From the French side, M. Pierre Dureau in his recollections of his stay at Trentham, emphasised the friendliness of the locals. His main complaint was the inclement weather which, on occasion, turned the camp into a sea of mud.[19] An enterprising Mrs Margaret Armitage and her mother sold toiletries, candles etc at the camp. She found the troops to be very friendly and used the occasions to practice her French. Mrs Armitage was employed by Williams Deacon Bank at the Central Clearing House but left in 1942 to join the WRNS.

From time to time, the legionnaires would be taken from the camp on training marches.

On one such occasion near panic was caused in the nearby Blurton area when a child, having seen soldiers marching toward him, ran to his parents screaming 'The Germans are coming!' Neighbours, however, on emerging from their homes were relieved to find that the approaching troops, whilst armed, were, in fact, of the French variety!

On 3rd July French warships in British ports were seized and their crews detained. This move was taken to prevent a possible German takeover of the French fleet following the armistice between France and Germany which came into effect on 25th June. The French naval personnel from those vessels were interned in a number of temporary camps, the majority of them, some 13,600, at Aintree. However, a number were transferred to Trentham Park.

Earlier, on 1st July, the 13th DBLE split and of the original 1619 survivors who had arrived at Trentham, some 636 officers and men boarded trains for Bristol to facilitate their eventual repatriation to North Africa. At this point, further tension arose at the camp when a guard of honour, comprising those who had rallied to de Gaulle, refused to present arms to their departing colleagues.[20] Local born legionnaire James Williamson returned that morning to Trentham Park from one of his nocturnal visits only to find that his battalion colleagues had left. On reporting to the British guard room, he was advised to 'clear off, burn your uniform and get some civilian clothes!' This he did, but subsequently joined the Berkshire Regiment and, later, the Parachute Regiment.[21]

A few days later, on 10th July, the remainder of the legionnaires of 13th DBLE left Trentham. Among these was M Pierre Dureau who recalls being transferred to Aldershot where a unit of the Foreign Legion which had already rallied to de Gaulle, was based. M Dureau and a number of his colleagues subsequently moved to Camberley where they participated in the formation of the Hadfield-Spears Ambulance Unit, an Anglo-French initiative which later did excellent work during the North Africa campaign.[22]

Whilst the remaining French managed to turn out an 'impeccable parade'[23] for a visit of King George VI on 25th August 1940, discipline had otherwise become rather lax in the Trentham Camp. From time to time inspections of this and other similar establishments were carried out by Free French officers to ascertain how recruitment to the movement was progressing, how morale was, etc. A report of such a visit on 13th September paints a picture of squalor, low morale and discontent and refers to the men, now mainly sailors and reservists, as 'unruly and unshaven.' After a few days the author of the report was officially put in charge of the camp under British supervision. As a first step towards alleviating the situation, he assembled the 1,700 men and divided them into companies of 100 under an officer and NCO's. The companies were then further divided into groups of 15 or 20 each with a leading seaman or corporal as leader. A military carving up of the day also ensued with roll calls and various activities. This soon got the men and the camp into better shape and they were eventually transformed from a *'rabble'* into *'some semblance of military dignity'*. A subsequent visit by an English Admiral found him pleasantly surprised, the men by that time being well drilled in best uniforms with an immaculate guard of honour. This was in complete contrast to the shambles that he had encountered during an earlier visit. As a result, on 11th October, the British guards were removed to enable the French to provide their own. This was regarded as a great honour and much appreciated by the French.[24]

Another report dated 12th September refers to a large number of personnel at Trentham who had elected to go home (rather than joining de Gaulle's Free French) requesting leave to 'find work in British industry.' Several presented themselves at the nearby Michelin factory, Stoke-on-Trent but were refused employment.[25] The reasoning behind this, no doubt, was that authorities at this time were extremely nervous about the likelihood of enemy or fifth column infiltrators. Also, the Michelin factory was working for national defence and some French sailors were understood to be pro-Nazi. There was also a problem at Trentham Park regarding a sailor who could not be accounted for, his name and details appearing to be unrecorded elsewhere. The situation was further intensified by rumours of invaders and agents etc following the discovery on 14th August of 17 parachutes in the Uttoxeter area.[26] Bombing had also occurred in the Stoke-on-Trent area on a number of occasions[27] and all this made the authorities extremely cautious. Some French sailors were, however, recruited into the Canadian army and navy at this period.

On 23rd September, those French officers remaining, being regulars and therefore pro-Nazi Vichy French (ie. not rallied to de Gaulle) were relieved of their posts and taken elsewhere to await repatriation. The men were assembled to say farewell and the officers urged them to *'remain well disciplined under their reserve officers'*. They were all to meet subsequently on board the repatriation ship 'Massilia' taking them to French North Africa.[28]

Finally, during the latter part of November 1940, the remaining French sailors left Trentham for repatriation by sea. The relevant entry in the records bears the comment that there was 'no difficulties of any sort and the moves were completed satisfactorily.'[29] Thus, this unique period in North Staffordshire's history came to a close.

NOTES

1. War diary of unit PRO 166/3771
2. Ibid
3. R. C. Anderson 'Devils, Not Men' Robert Hale p70
4. Ibid p73
5. Ex information Dr J.Delin
6. Ibid
7. Mr K.Gavin, a member of the Auxiliary Fire Service at the time recalls that on one occasion on returning from duty along Eccleshall Road (ie. at the rear of the park) he witnessed deer in front of his vehicle being chased by several legionnaires brandishing bayonets. Tradition has it that, after the war, compensation was paid to the Trentham Estate by the French Authorities for loss of deer. However, the writer has not traced any records to substantiate this.
8. J.Gunther 'Inside Europe Today' Hamish Hamilton p75
9. J.Lukas 'The Last European War' Routledge & Kegan Paul) p86
   NB-Dr J.Delin kindly supplied details of the relevant BBC Studio and timing of the broadcast.
10. Memo dated 27th June 1940 from the Prime Minister to First Lord of the Admiralty, quoted by Winston S.Churchill in 'The Second World War' Cassell Vol II p150
11. George Wigg 'Lord Wigg' Michael Joseph pp99/100
12. Ibid p101
13. D.Porch 'The French Foreign Legion' Macmillan p471
14. Sir Llewellyn Woodward 'British Foreign Policy in the Second World War' HMSO p77
15. Charles de Gaulle 'Memoires de Guerre' Plon, Paris Vol 1 p75
16. D.Porch op.cit p472
17. Ibid pp471/472
18. Defence Regulation 18B - the Home Secretary could make a detention order 'if satisfied with respect to any particular person that with a view to preventing him acting in a manner prejudicial to the public safety or the defence of the realm, it is necessary to do so.'
19. Ex information Dr J.Delin
20. D.Porch op.cit p473
21. This action resulted in Williamson being listed as a deserter by the Legion until officially discharged on 5th April 1966.
22 Ex information Dr J.Delin
23. D.Porch op.cit. p473
24. Ex information Dr J.Delin
25. Ibid
26. PRO WO166/1301
27. PRO WO166/94
28. Ex information Dr J.Delin
29. PRO WO166/1220 - this entry in the War Diary, West Lancs area Sept 1939-Dec 1941 under the sub-heading of No.2 Sub-Area Staffordshire, is dated 30th November 1940 and refers to 6,000 sailors leaving the area ie. as opposed to Trentham Park itself.

Chapter 6

The CCH - Staffing, Stage & Sport

'German planes in the skyway, their drone fills the air,
An alert has been sounded - why look! there's a flare.
Can you hear the bombs falling, see flashes, hear crumps?
'Tis the start of a fire-blitz - fall-in stirrup pumps!'

P S Quick Outcast Magazine Vol II p75

Against the background of the friendly 'invasion' by the French, the business of the Central Clearing House continued and at the end of August 1940 its first anniversary was celebrated. Amongst other things the event was marked by a formal presentation on 23rd August of impressive commemorative earthenware mugs by the Comptroller, Percy S. Quick, to all 'Outcasts' who were still members of the clearing staff.

The ware had been especially commissioned from Falcon Ware (T Lawrence Ltd) of Longton. The celebrations reached their climax on the following evening with a large party in the restaurant for which local artistes had been engaged to entertain.

The Outcasts' Commemorative Mug.   *T Symons*

However, events in Trentham were soon to be overshadowed by the nightly bombing raids that the Luftwaffe had commenced on the capital. Naturally the thoughts of the CCH staff who had transferred from London were very much with their relatives, friends and colleagues who remained there. The so called 'Blitz' was to continue until the Spring of 1941 and was part of an offensive by the Germans intended to paralyse the centre of Britain's administration and disable the London docks, etc. as a prerequisite to invasion. Night after night the air was filled with the bloodcurdling wail of sirens from soon after dusk, and the crash of anti-aircraft artillery and the whistle and crump of falling bombs would continue until dawn. Whole streets were levelled, including property belonging to 'Outcasts' and casualties mounted grievously whilst the night skies over London glowed red from fires in the city.

At Trentham, clearing staff quickly responded to an appeal for the Lord Mayor's London Air Raid Distress Fund with a donation of £65.14s 0d. Coincidentally, in The Outcast house journal, joint editors Guy Townsend and Norman Pile paid tribute to their London colleagues and wrote of *'their deep sympathy in the trials that they are undergoing and our sincere admiration for the splendid courage with which they are facing them. The citizens of embattled London are indeed writing a page of history which for mass stoicism and heroism transcends that of any other era and provides a fuller and finer example of the worth and meaning of the true democratic spirit that the world has yet seen.'*[1]

By the beginning of September there were both day and night Luftwaffe air offensives and bombings were no longer confined to the south east of England. They ranged far and wide over the rest of the country with Merseyside, Tyneside, Cardiff, Swansea, Bristol, Plymouth, Birmingham and the Midlands all taking their share of destruction. On 15th November a savage attack was launched on Coventry where much damage was done to the residential centre of the city and its famous cathedral. In recalling the event, a relative once informed me that *'there wasn't a minute's break for a solid 11 hours'*. A number of the former CCH staff can recall seeing the sky red from the flames following the Coventry bombing, particularly from the Rough Close area.

In October the CCH suffered its first and possibly only war casualty fatality. Mr L.A. Dupree, aged 44 years, of the Midland Bank staff was on Home Guard parade when he suffered a 'fainting fit.' In falling, he sustained a heavy blow on the head which resulted in a haemorrhage from which he never recovered. He was buried with full military honours at Newcastle-under-Lyme on 15th October.

The Autumn of 1940 saw the emergence of yet another important extension of the cultural activities at the Trentham CCH with the inception of Siren Theatre. Founded by Leonard Crainford, an employee of the Westminster Bank, the drama club quickly established itself on a basis which proved to be a permanent one. Siren Theatre was evolved after Crainford had noted that the London theatres had quickly responded to public demand by arranging lunch-time, tea-time or matinee performances as alternatives to those in the evenings when there were black-out conditions, or the likelihood of being disturbed by air raid warnings and night bombings. Crainford's proposal was to provide siren free entertainment on Sunday afternoons. In addition, the CCH Comptroller, Percy S Quick, realised that among those personnel evacuated from London, living for the main part in billets, there would be many who could occupy their leisure time and enjoy taking part or assisting in dramatic productions whilst coincidentally giving pleasure to others. The idea was to form a 'theatre show' with a difference - *'drama and drinking and entertainment and eating'*. The restaurant became the regular venue, and during the interval teas were served in the lounge surrounding the auditorium, for which tables could be reserved. Seats for the performance were 1s 3d, teas 9d, and the bar opened at the end of the performance. Pointing out that the *'task of beating the Beast of Berlin would necessitate maybe frequent changes in the times of habits'*, Crainford, in The Outcast journal, urged his colleagues to *'get the Siren Theatre habit'*.[2] Quick became an extremely active first President and an enthusiastic membership under Crainford's directorship soon established itself. The first production of Siren Theatre was given on Sunday 10th November. In this Crainford made his Trentham stage debut in Noel Coward's short play 'Fumed Oak', whilst the rest of the programme comprised Colin Byrd's comedy 'The Bathroom Tap' and Maurice Moseivitch's 'The Magic Suit'. A large audience attended and it is recorded that the performances were enthusiastically received. Subsequently. the same programme was presented at Stone Town Hall in aid of Spitfire funds.

According to Mrs L.R.Pennell, Leonard Crainford seemed misplaced in the banking world of the CCH, but he was *'brilliant on stage work and production'*. Sir Arthur Bryan also confirms that Crainford was *'extremely dedicated to the theatre'*. Having truly laid the foundations, it is to Crainford's credit that no matter the changes in personnel or those in the tastes of audiences, the demand to see Siren Theatre productions continued until 1946 when hostilities had ceased and the CCH returned to London. Crainford also became an advisor for Sunday evening concerts which were regularly held as part of the war-time entertainment at the Victoria Hall, Hanley.[3]

During this period, the 'Outcasts' were becoming more involved in the various aspects of community life of North Staffordshire. For example, on Sunday 10th November, CCH personnel participated in the Remembrance Parade at Stoke-on-Trent wearing their uniforms which represented various local units including the Home Guard, St John Ambulance Brigade etc.[4] It is also recorded that, at this time, the CCH staff made a 'substantial' contribution to the Lord Mayor of Stoke-on-Trent's Spitfire Fund.[5] Dennis Morris also recalls staff from the CCH organising parties for the children which included all types of games which were 'foreign' to the area. On the sporting front, use was made of local facilities and links continued to be forged with other clubs in the area. For example, the Athletics Section held competitions against North Staffs Harriers at the Michelin Sports Ground, cricket matches were played against such teams as Abbotsholme School and the Royal Military College of Science, Hartshill whilst the football team's opponents included Burslem Albion and Mossfield Colliery. The ladies hockey team played against Lotus and Stoke Municipal Officers whilst the men pitched their skills against the likes of RAF Meir and the Royal Worcester Regiment. In

Leonard Crainford
Director of Entertainments

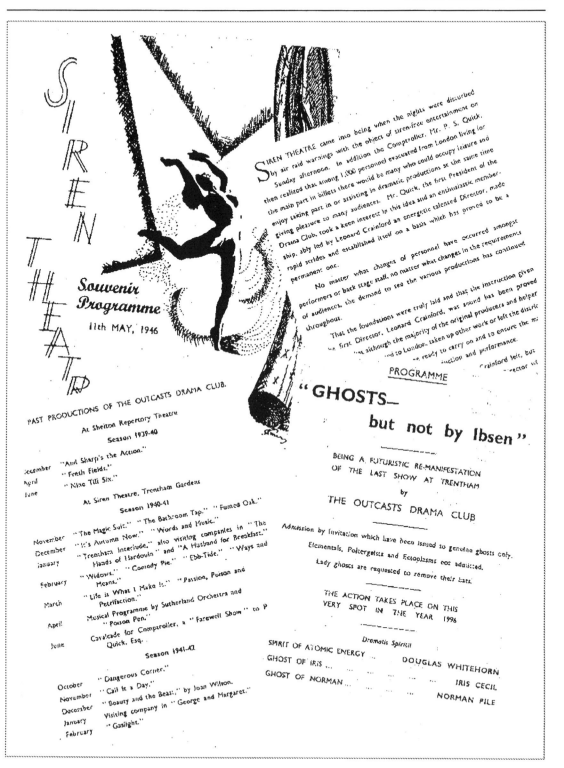

S I R E N T H E A T R

Souvenir Programme
11th MAY, 1946

SIREN THEATRE came into being when the nights were disturbed by air raid warnings with the object of siren-free entertainment on Sunday afternoon. In addition the Comptroller, Mr. P. S. Quick, then realized that among 1,000 personnel evacuated from London living for the main part in or assisting in dramatic productions at the same time enjoy taking part in billets there would be many who could occupy leisure and giving pleasure to many audiences. Mr. Quick, the first President of the Drama Club, took a keen interest in this idea and an enthusiastic member ship, ably led by Leonard Crainford an energetic talented Director, made rapid strides and established itself on a basis which has proved to be a permanent one.

No matter what changes of personnel have occurred amongst performers or back stage staff, no matter what changes in the requirements of audiences, the demand to see the various productions has continued throughout.

That the foundations were truly laid and that the instruction given by first Director, Leonard Crainford, was sound has been proved ... although the majority of the original producers and helper ... to London, taken up other work or left the distric ... ready to carry on and to ensure the m ... action and performance.
Crainford left, but ... ector wi

PAST PRODUCTIONS OF THE OUTCASTS DRAMA CLUB.

At Shelton Repertory Theatre
Season 1939-40

December	"And Sharp's the Action."
April	"Fresh Fields."
June	"Nine Till Six."

At Siren Theatre, Trentham Gardens
Season 1940-41

November	"The Magic Suit." "The Bathroom Tap." "Fumed Oak."
December	"It's Autumn Now." "Words and Music."
January	"Trentham Interlude." also visiting companies in "The Hands of Hardouin" and "A Husband for Breakfast."
February	"Widows." "Comedy Pie." "Ebb-Tide." "Ways and Means."
March	"Life is What I Make It." "Passion, Poison and Petrifaction."
April	Musical Programme by Sutherland Orchestra and "Poison Pen."
June	Cavalcade for Comptroller, a "Farewell Show" to P Quick, Esq.

Season 1941-42

October	"Dangerous Corner."
November	"Call It a Day."
December	"Beauty and the Beast." by Joan Wilson.
January	Visiting company in "George and Margaret."
February	"Gaslight."

PROGRAMME

"GHOSTS—

but not by Ibsen"

BEING A FUTURISTIC RE-MANIFESTATION OF THE LAST SHOW AT TRENTHAM
by
THE OUTCASTS DRAMA CLUB

Admission by invitation which have been issued to genuine ghosts only.
Elementals, Poltergeists and Ectoplasms not admitted.
Lady ghosts are requested to remove their hats.

THE ACTION TAKES PLACE ON THIS VERY SPOT IN THE YEAR 1996

Dramatis Spiritit

SPIRIT OF ATOMIC ENERGY	DOUGLAS WHITEHORN
GHOST OF IRIS	IRIS CECIL
GHOST OF NORMAN	NORMAN PILE

61

addition to those fixtures, inter-Bank competitions were frequently held for most sports and it was also not unusual for CCH players to turn out for local teams such as Stoke RFC.

To further counteract the boredom of depressing dark, and frequently wet, winter Sunday afternoons, tea dances were held in the restaurant. These events were organised by the Self-Entertainments Committee and were an immediate success, possibly on account of the presence of live bands. Commencing at 3pm, the functions generally continued until 8.30pm but it was not unusual for the band to be retained for a further 1 1/2 hours when there was *'no evidence of dancers wishing to leave'*.

Christmas 1940 brought a lull in the air war. Speculating, the local Evening Sentinel observed that this may have resulted from bad weather conditions or, alternatively, Hitler's hope that if the Luftwaffe did not bomb Britain, then the RAF would not retaliate by bombing Germany during the festive season. In fact the RAF were grounded on Christmas Day, but bombing crews resumed their missions as soon as weather conditions improved.[6] At Trentham a number of events were held to celebrate the festive period but the most popular appear to have been a children's party and a carol concert. Attended by Father Christmas, the party appears to have had all the atmosphere and trimmings despite the stringencies of war. Entertainment was also provided by the respected puppeteers, the Bowman Bros, whose family had been associated with Punch & Judy shows since 1886. The carol concert on Sunday afternoon, 22nd December, was given in the restaurant by the Outcasts' Choir under the direction of Alfred Pinnington. An organ was especially installed for the occasion and the choral items included Gounod's 'Bethlehem' and Quilter's 'Non nobis domine' in addition to the usual carols. Prior to this, carol singers had also toured the various sections of the CCH during office hours and collected donations for the Red Cross funds.

'Supreme courage in our coming victory and a continued spirit of courage and cheerfulness in the face of wartime difficulties and perils' was the keynote of the New Year message in the Evening Sentinel.[7] Whilst the German air offensive of the past few months had caused much more damage and disruption than was admitted, it had not succeeded in its objective of destroying the RAF's fighter strength, nor the British morale. Spirits were certainly high as the 'Outcasts' celebrated their second New Years Eve at Trentham with a *'rattling good dance and cabaret'*. With dancing to the Sutherland Band, the function commenced at 6.30pm but, due to war - time conditions, concluded at 10.30pm with the customary Auld Lang Syne. A report of the event notes that Hitler too must have been celebrating, *'as there were no unwelcome guests!'*[8]

The continuation of the war brought staffing implications for the CCH and, indeed, for Banks in general. Personnel were continually being called to the colours whilst coincidentally at Trentham a small number, for personal or private reasons, wished to return to the capital. As a consequence, almost from the beginning, locals had been recruited in an effort to alleviate the situation. Nevertheless, whilst recruitment had, up to this period, been generally maintained to peacetime standards, it was becoming clear that such levels would be inadequate. However, the staffing situation was to become more acute later in that year when new Government measures were announced extending the age band for the call-up of males (ie. downwards to $18\frac{1}{2}$ years and upwards to 50), together with the conscription of single women between the ages of 20 and 30 years.[9] However, a number of the female staff at Trentham had already resigned to join the services, even before conscription was announced. Having earlier witnessed the bronzed figures of the Chasseurs Alpins troops in their midst, Mrs Jean Butler (nee Wright) of the National Provincial staff, and a number of her female colleagues, were persuaded that they should leave their 'boring' jobs and join the WAAF or similar, which they ultimately did. They were not alone. At this time women generally were, in a way, experiencing a form of liberation, a situation which they would not have undergone in peace time. According to tradition they had been raised and educated to marry and provide children and, suddenly, they were made aware of other opportunites, many volunteering for war work etc. This added to the staffing problems at Trentham and in 1941 a number of local girls under the age of 16 years were engaged to replace staff. Yet even this measure proved to be inadequate and it subsequently became necessary to recruit both boys and girls of 14 years of age.[10] In 1941, 316 members of staff were recruited locally as against 123 in the previous year.[11]

It is also perhaps worth noting that at this time it proved difficult to obtain labour to carry out internal decoration at Trentham. The restaurant, in particular, was in need of painting and this was undertaken by members of the CCH staff who volunteered for the work.[12]

Fred Powell joined the CCH at the age of 14 years, commencing duties as a messenger boy with the Midland Bank. He enjoyed the working environment at Trentham and the social aspect. Like his colleagues, he took advantage of the free facilities including the famous swimming baths and use of the rowing boats on the lake. Whilst being unable to recall the precise details of his salary, he nevertheless is able to confirm that he received a 'good bonus' at Christmas, and that his conditions of service included free lunches.

Another potential source of staff for the CCH was the Banks in the North Staffordshire area. For example, transferring from the Stoke-on-Trent branch of Barclays enabled Sir Arthur Bryan to earn an extra ten shillings per week, 'a large amount at that time' he recalled. Being the first local male to join Barclays Section he, like Fred Powell, enjoyed his time at Trentham, a period which he regarded as one of the most important in his life. Not only did he met his future wife, Betty, at Trentham (she being one of the original London staff) but he contends that working with such 'well educated and intelligent colleagues' broadened his experience which he was able to take advantage of in later years. A part-time member of the CCH Fire Brigade, Sir Arthur also participated in the social side. He particularly admired the way in which the 'Outcasts' entered into the life of Stoke-on-Trent and felt that they made an enormous contribution to the area as a whole. In once admiring the apparent many talents of his colleagues he recalled that one quipped - 'we have such boring jobs, we have to have other interests!' But until he joined the RAF in 1942, Sir Arthur felt it a privilege to work with such people whom he described as a 'force for the good'.

Another local recruit was Miss E J Yorke, who joined Barclays Section at the CCH. Whilst commencing duties a little later than her colleagues quoted earlier, she nevertheless spoke with affection of the 'great times' at Trentham. Her duties included sorting cheques during which she stood for most of the day, but otherwise she operated Recordak and comptometer machines. Miss Yorke enjoyed her working period at Trentham, 'never having had the chance to get bored!'

Notable among the CCH staff departures in 1941 was that of the Comptroller, Percy Quick. His departure on 27th June on being appointed as Assistant General Manager of Barclays was considered by many to be in fitting recognition of 'his ability and efficiency in so successfully having devised and established' the CCH. The house journal records the occasion as being a memorable one and such was the esteem and affection in which he was held, the CCH suspended operations temporarily to bid farewell to its Chief. Special tribute was paid to Mr Quick's keen interest in the welfare of the staff and to his encouragement of all sections of the CCH's many social pursuits in which he himself had been most actively involved. Following this, he was presented with a Spode china dinner service and a coffee service, a Minton china tea service and an illuminated address on behalf of all sections of the CCH.

In the evening a special entertainment - 'Cavalcade for Comptroller' was held attended by over 500 members of staff. A cast of 70 under the direction of Leonard Crainford performed selections from previous productions staged by the 'Outcasts' since 1939. All profits from the evening were donated to the Bank Clerks' Orphanage.[13]

A frequent contributor to The Outcast magazine, Quick recorded his thoughts on leaving Trentham in the following short poem which he entitled *'Farewell'*:

Rumours of war, the reason for our meeting, Friends,
Became established fact ere one short week had passed:
Meanwhile the scheme created for these very ends
Was coaxed to practice on a basis wrought to last.

Since then, much water 'neath old London Bridge has flowed
And many a Nazi bomb has scarred dear London's face,
While we have found some surcease from war's heavy load
In Trentham Village - peaceful, lovely, rural place.

Strangers at first, but now a fellowship of friends,
Each out to help the other in the daily task,
Thus, every benefit co-operation lends,
Accrues to all - for more, there is no need to ask.

Change comes with time and many of our men have left
To take their places in the serried ranks of war;
Girls too, have gone, our family has been bereft:
The call is answered - duty done - who can do more?

Their work is done by local lads and lasses,
Many have joined us as the months have slid away.
Our outlook, may it teach them as time passes-
That Outcast fellowship means something day by day.

Words fail one when the time arrives for leaving,
But heart and memory will not falter, which is well.
I part from you with true paternal grieving,
And in salute would wish you all -
Good Luck! Farewell![14]

Percival S Quick -
The CCH's first comptroller

Quick's successor as Comptroller was Derbyshire born Brian Holme Bennett. Having transferred from the post of Assistant Staff Manager of the Midland Bank, he proved a worthy replacement and he remained at Trentham until the CCH returned to the capital in 1946. A keen golfer, Bennett had seen service in the First World War, attaining the rank of Second Lieutenant and at one period had served in the original Tank Corps.[15] Mrs L R Pennell recalls Mr Bennett as a *'portly man, friendly and of the "hail fellow well met" variety'*.

Aside from these matters, culture continued to feature heavily on the agenda at Trentham. From time to time Leonard Crainford was instrumental in arranging for visiting artistes to perform at the CCH, under the auspices of the Council for Encouragement of Music & the Arts (CEMA). Set up in 1940 with the intention of giving the arts a fighting chance in wartime, the Council organised ballet, opera, drama, recitals and orchestral concerts all over the country at all forms of venues including factories. According to Angus Calder, the public found it harder to use what spare time they had during this period and they were willing to venture their earnings on such events to give them a try. They provided a form of escapism from the war and thousands were attracted to music for the first time.[16] Notable among the CEMA concerts visiting the CCH in 1941 was that by the English Singers. The famous quartet (comprising Flora Mann, Lillian Berger, Norman Stone and Julian Were) with Reginald Paul (piano) visited Trentham as part of a nation-wide tour.[17] Other artistes who visited the CCH during this period under the auspices of CEMA were the pianist Arthur Rubinstein and the Newcastle String Orchestra under the direction of H.Leslie Jones with well known local contralto Dora Capey. It is also worth noting that such events were attended by large numbers, even when in competition with a brilliant summer's evening.

Notwithstanding the professional visits, the 'Outcasts' continued to delight audiences with their own amateur drama productions and concerts. In fact, even the new Comptroller Brian Bennett was heard to remark that he had not witnessed such 'slick' professional productions from amateurs. Notable productions of Siren Theatre during 1941 included 'Poison Pen' by Richard Llewellyn, Dodie Smith's comedy 'Call it a day' and J.B.Priestley's 'Dangerous Corner'. In October the players took their production of 'Dangerous Corner' to the Cheshire Joint Sanatorium at Loggerheads. Here the play was staged in the establishments well equipped theatre/dining hall and those patients who were unable to attend were able to listen to the performance via headphones.[18]

As for the Outcasts' Choral Society, they too performed at a number of external venues during the year under their conductor Alfred Pinnington. These included a music festival at St Giles Parish Church, Newcastle-under-Lyme on 29th May and also at St Andrew's Church, Westlands on 11th September. The reputation which the Society had already acquired in the area was such that large numbers attended. Another performance of the period worthy of mention was that of Edward German's 'Tom Jones' on 30th April 1941 at Trentham with Harry Vincent, founder of the famous Etruscan Choral Society, singing the exacting role of Tom. Etruria born Vincent was an official of CEMA and in 1947 he was awarded the MBE for his services to the organisation. The highlight of the year for the Outcasts' Choral Society, however, was their well attended concert at the Victoria Hall, Hanley on 28th December with guest soloists Leon Goosens (oboe) and Florence Austral (soprano). The choir, as usual, was under the direction of Alfred Pinnington with accompanists Leslie Jones (organ) and Pilot Officer (Dr) Leon Forrester (piano). Among the items rendered by the Choir were 'Come and thank him' from Bach's Christmas Oratorio whilst Florence Austral performed Mozart's 'Alleluia.' The distinguished Leon Goosens delighted the audience with his performances of Purcell's 'Air & Hornpipe' and Teleman's Sonata in G minor. Of the concert, Geoffrey Thompson, the highly respected but tough music critic of the Evening Sentinel wrote *'although the choir, like many, is suffering from shortage of male singers, it is clearly a well trained body of singers and its artistic treatment of all the music gave very real pleasure.'*[19] All proceeds from the concert were donated to the Lord Mayor's War Comforts Fund.

On the sporting front the year's successes included the cricket team's victories against BTH, Meece and Trentham and those of the ladies tennis teams against Cobridge Ladies and Trentham Ladies (twice). An inter-bank 'splash' took place at Trentham's famous 132ft long swimming baths on 2nd August. Lying in a natural valley and served by a miniature railway, the pool was popular with the locals and CCH staff alike. This event proved to be no exception, being well attended and providing a good afternoon's entertainment. Generally, however, whilst a number of inter-bank competitions continued, the number of fixtures appears to have decreased, the house journal citing the call-up as a reason, not to mention the weather. The magazine appealed for new members of the Sports Club or 'for a greater show of enthusiasm by present members'.

Christmas 1941 had a tendency to be overshadowed by events of earlier that month in the Far East. On 8th December Britain, jointly with the United States, had declared war on Japan and two days later the tragic sinking by the Japanese of the battleship HMS Prince of Wales and the battle-cruiser HMS Repulse off Malaya was announced. Fortunately, escorting destroyers did manage to save 2,000 officers and men out of 2,800 of the ships' crews.[20] The only good news on the war front appeared to be that Rommel's troops in North Africa were on the run.[21]

War or not, Christmas without a pantomime was unthinkable! Not to be outdone by the local Theatre Royal, Hanley, the CCH's Siren Theatre stole a march on that establishment by staging a panto of its own on 12th December - 'Beauty & the Beast'. However, they were ably assisted by members of the Theatre Royal's orchestra for the occasion! The result was an outstanding triumph for Joan Wilson, who had written the book, lyrics and music, and producer Leonard Crainford. Two days later the cast gave a special repeat performance for the children of CCH staff. This was followed by an early appearance of Father Christmas who distributed presents.[22]

Frank Bovis's drawing of the Procenium and Stage

A special gala dance was held in the gaily decorated restaurant on 23rd December featuring the dance cabaret band of the Royal Netherlands Brigade (Princess Irene's).[23] Subsequently, at the same venue, 300 'Outcasts' celebrated the passing of the old year and the arrival of the new with the aid of the dance band of the South Lancashire Fusiliers. Just before midnight the following lines, especially written for the occasion by Joan Wilson, were read by Leonard Crainford:

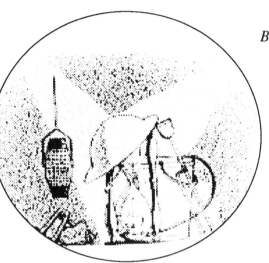

'New Year's Eve. Let us for a moment
Leave our fun and jollity to give
A moment's thought to those who should
Be with us now, for is it not a solemn time?
Let us for a moment think
Not solely of the fact that soon
Another year is born. But rather
Let us think of those whose sacrifice
Has made it possible for us
To meet together, and with peace of mind
Enjoy the ancient rite of watching
One year die, and its successor
Usher in another lease of life.
Let us think of men who for our sakes
Must see the bodies of their fellow men
Crushed into the desert's burning sands.
Of those who with the same ideal of freedom
Force the Nazi terror back across the icy plains.
And let our part in this now world-wide strife
Be no mere service to their bravery,
But rather let us keep in mind the goal
For which they strive - the Brotherhood of man,
And let us play our part, that this New Year
May raise the curtain on the final scene
Of this most grim and bloody tragedy.
And let us hope that e'er another year is
Born, it may be said
They did not fight in vain,
They gave us liberty.'[24]

69

Following the striking of twelve on a gong and the customary 'Auld Lang Syne,' 1941 was bid adieu and the New Year ushered in. Generally, however, New Year's Eve was a quiet occasion in North Staffordshire with the Evening Sentinel reporting that 'scenes of revelry, customary in peacetime, were almost missing'.[25]

NOTES
1. The Outcast Vol I. p229
2. Ibid. p278
3. Ibid. p309
4. Ibid. p308
5. Ibid. p281
6. Evening Sentinel 27th December 1940
7. Ibid, 1st January 1941
8. The Outcast Vol I. p372
9. Evening Sentinel 2nd December 1941
10. F W Hindmarsh op.cit. pp73/74
11. Ibid p73
12. The Outcast Vol II p271
13. Ibid. pp166/168
14. Ibid. p140
15. Ibid. pp156/158
16. Angus Calder 'The People's War' Pimlico p373
17. The Outcast Vol II. p141
18. Ibid. p287
19. Evening Sentinel 29th December 1941
20. The crew of the Repulse included former 'Outcast' Ken Brown(Barclays) who was not originally listed among the survivors. However, he did survive the tragic sinking. The Outcast Vol II pp344 & 380
21. Evening Sentinel 18th December 1941
22. The Outcast Vol II pp353 & 358
23. Ibid. p385
24. Ibid. pp393/4
25. Evening Sentinel 1st January 1942

Additional artwork by John Emery, taken from the 1940-41 "Siren Theatre" programme.

Chapter 7
Pinnington & the Ceramic City Choir

'The German invasion may, or may not come-
but nothing can stop the march of the snowdrops."

Firefly The Outcast Vol II p3

In January 1942 victory seemed to be no closer with the news appearing to be a constant, depressing recital of defeats and deprivations. As if this were not enough to contend with, a major disaster occurred in North Staffordshire on New Years Day, this being a huge explosion at Sneyd Colliery. The death toll was 57, the victims ranging from boys aged 16 years to veteran miners. Such was the scale of the catastrophe that 9 rescue teams were involved. According to a contemporary report in the Evening Sentinel, the disaster was the *'worst to hit the mother town of the Potteries, with Burslem and the surrounding district in mourning.'*[1] The Lord Mayor of Stoke-on-Trent (Alderman H.W. McBrine) immediately announced the launch of a fund for the relief of dependents of those who had lost their lives and, within a few days, a sum of £11,000 had been raised. Among the first donations listed was a sum of £57 from staff of the CCH, Trentham.[2] According to The Outcast magazine, the staff, *'as part of the community of North Staffordshire, were deeply grieved to learn of the accident at Sneyd Colliery involving, as it did, the loss of so many valuable lives.'* A number of the CCH staff having had the opportunity of visiting pits in the district and seeing the miner at work, had gained *'a fuller appreciation of the dangerous and arduous business of coal getting'*. Such was the feeling at the CCH, Trentham that member of staff D.C.G Whitehorn personally visited the Lord Mayor and presented the sum collected on behalf of his colleagues.[3]

If there was an antidote to relieve depressed spirits at this time, it was to be found in music. At least a number of people in North Staffordshire shared that view. As Paul Anderton observed - 'choral works, especially those with a powerful grip on the emotions of working people brought up in the chapel tradition, could be overwhelming in their psychological impact at such time of community distress.'[4] Music, and in particular choral singing, already popular in the area, was in a way, a weapon. It was a form of escapism which, coincidentally, could be used to rebuild morale and inspire national pride.

Following a concert on 15th January at the Victoria Hall, Hanley at which Dr (later Sir) Malcolm Sargent conducted the London Philharmonic Orchestra, local businessman Charles Henry Tildesley conceived the idea of a local choir to match *'the splendour of the orchestra'*. This resulted in the formation of the Ceramic City Choir which, to this day, remains an integral part of North Staffordshire's culture. The choir's first concert, consisting of a performance of Handel's 'Messiah,' was given on 14th April. The chosen venue was the same Victoria Hall, Hanley and some 270 selected choristers participated. Sargent conducted the performance, he having agreed to become the choir's permanent conductor, and Alfred Pinnington of the CCH, Trentham was its first Hon. Chorus Master.

Dr Malcolm Sargent at rehearsal with Alfred Pinnington
Evening Sentinel

An original 'Outcast', Alfred Henry Pinnington was one of Barclay's senior officials. Born in Highbury, London it soon became evident that he had inherited his father's love of music and, at the age of 7, his voice training commenced. He was fortunate to become a chorister of St.Margaret's Church, Westminster during the period that the organist & choirmaster was Edwin H. Lemare (1865-1934) who, by the age of 34, had been widely acclaimed as the greatest living English organist. Lemare's choir of 20 men and 40 boys was one of the finest in London and under his charge, St Margaret's gained a reputation for music of 'surpassing quality'.[5] There is no doubt that the period under the direction of Lemare had a profound influence on young Pinnington which was to be of advantage later in life but also more immediately when he moved to the choir of the Chapel Royal, St.James'. Here he attained the position of leading choir boy and had the honour of singing at the Coronation of King Edward VII. When his voice eventually broke, he went on to study the organ. Subsequently, Pinnington served in the First World War but as a result of wounds received, he was hospitalised until 1920.[6]

According to Sir Arthur Bryan, Pinnington had intended to make music his profession, but the extent of his war wounds, including mutilation of the fingers, unfortunately precluded this.

Remembered as a 'big' man, Pinnington - 'Pin' or 'Pinny' to his close friends - was respected not only for his undoubted musical ability, but also for his wit and 'good natured charm of manner' which endeared him to all those with whom he came into contact. Having observed him at rehearsals, John Summers commented - *'the whole proceedings are always entertaining. With jacket and pullover discarded and baton held aloft, he encourages, rebukes and with expressive hands, as it were, caresses the singers into giving their most sensitive expression to the music.'*[7]

Prior to evacuation to Trentham Pinnington was, amongst other things, a member of the Royal Choral Society and, as such, acquainted with Malcolm Sargent. Some tend to believe that it was as a consequence of this that Sargent agreed to become permanent conductor of the Ceramic City Choir. This may be so but, in any event, as Paul Anderton points out, Sargent at that time was engaged in a personal war-time effort to secure work for musicians. He had a reputation for inspiring amateur singers and so the newly formed choir became *'another of his musical offsprings'*.[8] There is no doubt, however, that the appointment of Malcolm Sargent as permanent conductor to the choir had a number of advantages. For example, he was very popular, having considerable appeal with audiences. In addition, his connections ensured attendances of first class artistes at Ceramic City Choir concerts and over the next few years audiences were to see and hear some of the finest including Joan Hammond (soprano), Heddle Nash (tenor), Kathleen Ferrier (contralto), Gladys Ripley (contralto), Parry Jones (tenor), and Moisewitsch (piano), to name but a few. Moreover, the choir's repertoire was to include the likes of Mendelssohn's 'Elijah', Berlioz' 'Damnation of Faust', Verdi's 'Requiem', Handel's 'Judas Maccabeus' etc. By 1945, the choir's reputation was such that it had made its debut with BBC Radio.

To ensure first class performances from the choir, however, required team effort with weeks of rehearsals under Pinnington's baton, but it seems that a successful formula was achieved, for the choir went from success to success. Pinnington had, in any event, already become recognised in North Staffordshire music circles prior to his connections with the Ceramic City Choir, his concerts with the Outcasts' Choral Society attracting large audiences. It was fortunate for North Staffordshire and the CCH in particular that Pinnington's duties detained him at Trentham until the end of the war.

The last part of Pinnington's period with the Ceramic City Choir was extremely successful. Of the choir's performance of 'The Messiah' on 4th April 1945, contemporary editions of the local newspaper record the quality of choral singing as being *'on a very high level'*. Pinnington, together with Malcolm Sargent, received ovations from the capacity audience, and the Evening Sentinel music critic Geoffrey Thompson proclaimed *'one still marvels at the crispness and clarity of the singing he draws from the choir so large that in less hands it would be unwieldy.'*[9] Of that same performance the columnist 'Observer' in somewhat lighter vein commented - *'even the cat which mounted the steps leading up to the platform during the performance stopped dead in its tracks at one exciting moment then settled down comfortably for a quarter of an hour listening!'*[10] Later that year, on 20th September, Pinnington himself conducted the Ceramic City Choir, sharing the platform with contralto Kathleen Ferrier and oboist Leon Goosens. Whilst the rehearsals did not appear to be proceeding as successfully as Pinnington might have wished for a few days earlier, it nevertheless came right on the night with the press reporting that *'Pinnington got some first class singing from the choir.'*[11]

The choir's performance of 'The Messiah' on 25th April 1946 was, according to Geoffrey Thompson, *'the best for many years. Indeed'*, he continued, *'I have no personal recollection of a better "Messiah" performance anywhere else, not even those given by Beecham 16 or 17 years ago.'* With soloists Kathleen Ferrier (contralto), Robert Easton (bass), Ceinwen Rowlands (soprano), and Edgar Evans (tenor) the Evening Sentinel reported the Victoria Hall as being 'crowded to the doors'. But, according to Geoffrey Thompson, *'pride of place among Dr. Sargent's collaborators must be given to the choir of which the chorus master - Pinnington - has made a superb instrument.'*[12] It was perhaps befitting that this was the last such performance to be rehearsed by Pinnington before he and his colleagues at the CCH returned to the capital.

NOTES
1.   Evening Sentinel 1st and 2nd January 1942
2.   Ibid 13th January 1942
3.   The Outcast Vol II p394
4.   Paul Anderton 50 years of song 1942-1992 Ceramic City Choir p12
5.   N.Bardon 'Edwin H.Lemare' in The American Organist March 1986 p50
6.   J.Summers - Interview with A.H.Pinnington in The Outcast Vol I pp28/30
7.   Ibid p28
8.   Paul Anderton op.cit p9
9.   Evening Sentinel 5th April 1945
10. Ibid 6th April 1945 NB 'Observer' was the Sentinel's editor Ernest Newey Scott. Scott became a local institution and his 'Observer' column was eagerly read for its satirical content and witty dissection of the local scene.
11. Ibid 21st September 1945
12. Ibid 26th April 1946

Chapter 8
1942 & the Departure of Leonard Crainford

'We're free, you & I, to do as we choose,
A picture, a theatre, and nothing to lose.
We're free, you & I, to say what we like
About blasted Hitler - the so & so tyke!'

Anon. The Outcast Vol III p240

During the winter of 1942 with its deep snow, blizzards and very icy conditions, staff at the CCH, Trentham were fortunate in being able to temporarily forget the war and weather by attending numerous recreational pursuits after working hours. These included diverse activities such as inter-Bank general knowledge competitions and a series of lectures given by G F Hodgkin covering such subjects as 'Food and rationing' and 'The problem of reconstruction', etc. Competitions were also held to test the speed and accuracy of the 'Burroughs' adding machine operators. For the more culturally inclined outings were organised to the Theatre Royal, Hanley with a party of 200 travelling to see Tyrone Guthrie's production of Chekov's 'The Cherry Orchard'. On other occasions, a number of the staff visited the theatre for the Vic Wells Opera Company productions of 'Rigoletto' and 'La Traviata'. In addition, the Outcasts' Musical Society gave a concert in the restaurant featuring Stanford's 'Songs of the Sea' whilst the Siren Theatre entertained with such plays as Patrick Hamilton's Victorian thriller 'Gaslight', the comedy 'Yellow Sands' and a variety show entitled 'Sirenentertainment'. A number of dances were held in the restaurant featuring, amongst others, bands of the Royal Netherlands Brigade and RAF, Stafford.[1]

On Good Friday, a number of the CCH staff attended Trentham Church for the service. A large congregation heard the Outcasts' Choral Society conducted by Alfred Pinnington perform Stainer's 'God so loved the World'. An alternative service was subsequently arranged by the Vicar of Trentham, the Rev A G Grimes, for those who had to work and had missed their customary devotions. Pinnington was again in action when, at the beginning of May, he conducted a special concert at Trentham of the Outcasts' Choral Society, on this occasion using a baton which had been presented to him by Malcolm Sargent. Soloists included Dora Capey (contralto), Henry Bull (bass), and Ralph Jack (violin) with accompaniment by Leslie Jones. Of Pinnington's performance the house journal commented - *'he is of a professional class, we are extremely fortunate.'*[2]

In the CCH itself the problem of staffing persisted as the war continued, so much so that in the Spring of 1942 the Editors of The Outcast journal saw fit to comment that *'this institution of national importance is now being maintained by local staff to a degree which was certainly not envisaged at its inception.'* This was as a consequence of a considerable number of the remaining male staff being conscripted into HM Forces, whilst coincidentally others were returning to Head Office to relieve pressure there. But the Editors further observed - *'we now have an overwhelming preponderance of younger members of the gentler and, we observe, more beautiful sex!'*[3] In fact records do confirm that at this period the establishment of 987 staff consisted of 719 females and 268 males. Of these, 466 had been recruited locally.[4]

At the beginning of July the Siren Theatre (and indeed the CCH itself) was to experience a sad loss with the departure of its energetic and talented Director, Leonard Crainford to the Council for the Encouragement of Music & the Arts (CEMA). An official of the Westminster Bank, Crainford was an outstanding example of a person naturally given to organisation and to entertainment of others who willingly gave up his time to provide a form of escapism which people badly needed at this time. Siren Theatre, of which Crainford was the inspiration, had already served to entertain not only members of the CCH staff, but also thousands throughout the Potteries area and its foundations were so sound that the high standard of production and performance was to continue until the end of the war. Prior to his departure Crainford was invited to address local Rotarians and chose as his subject 'The Theatre and the Community'. In this he advocated the establishment of a Civic Theatre in the Potteries, citing Siren Theatre as an example.[5]

However, whilst being held in awe by some, Crainford, like so many theatrical directors, was not without his critics. For example, Alfred Pinnington, the conductor of the Outcasts' Choral Society, acted in a number of Crainford's productions and he felt that the Siren Theatre programmes might have been better served by longer plays instead of a number of small one act shows. Otherwise, he was of the opinion that the activity fulfilled a real need and found rehearsals 'such good fun'.[6] Others felt that more comedies should be presented, citing John Summer's production of Dodie Smith's 'Call it a day' as one of the most successful shows staged by Siren Theatre.

In answering his critics, Crainford stated that *'choosing plays for any audience is a difficult task and many things have to be taken into account. If we only presented two shows a year here at Trentham, the same type of play may be chosen each time. In Siren Theatre, however, we present a series of plays spread over seven months. This programme needs planning and working out with the same care and expert knowledge that is given to preparing a concert programme, a variety show or may I say, the menus*

of a hotel. How boring would an entire programme of comedies be! A tenor singing love songs all the evening would soon pall. If our favourite meal was set before us each time we needed to eat we should soon begin to refuse it.
This is why Siren Theatre's bill should be thought of as a whole. The list has variety, contrast, new features and there is something for everyone's taste.' He continued - 'there are a lot of other things which strongly influence the choice of plays today. There is a war on and we have already lost a number of men to the Forces and more are under notice. The supply of all materials necessary for the staging of plays is very restricted and some are quite impossible to obtain. They cost much more too. Labour costs also are certainly not less. Our stage itself imposes many limitations.'*

Nevertheless, whilst attempting to explain the difficulties which beset the path of the 'chooser of plays', Crainford hoped that patrons would appreciate the problems and continue to 'pack the house' for performances.[7]

Crainford's departure from Trentham was marked by an official presentation on 9th July of a 'substantial' cheque from colleagues, friends and well-wishers. In his address the Comptroller, Brian Bennett, paid tribute to Crainford of whose departure, he forecast, would be 'one of the milestones' when the history of the House was placed on record. In his reply, Crainford openly admitted that, prior to Trentham, he had not entered into the social life of his Bank but had since realised what he had missed from friendships, etc. Trentham, he concluded, had left a very great mark and the three years he had spent there had been among the happiest of his life.[8]

On the following evening the Outcasts' Drama Club paid a final tribute to Crainford by staging a review at which he was the guest of honour. Produced by Nancy Hines, 'Leonine Levites' was, according to the house journal, an event which provided *'the large and enthusiastic gathering with an evening packed full of delightful entertainment'.*[9] Nancy Hines went on to succeed Crainford and Bill Humphreys, a former player, recalls her as being *'very firm at rehearsals but indefatigable - a Joyce Grenfell type of person'.* Under her directorship, Siren Theatre continued to be one of the CCH's most successful ambassadors.

As the Autumn approached, with reports of Rommel's forces under 'heavy bombardment' and the 'greatest battle of the year' in progress south west of Stalingrad, a National Day of Prayer was observed on 3rd September in accordance with His Majesty's wishes. Church and open air services were held throughout the country while millions listened to a short service broadcast by the BBC at 11am. For 15 minutes, the wheels of industry were still, with office and shop workers also pausing in their labours.

At Trentham a short service was held at the CCH conducted by the Rev A.E. Grimes, Vicar of Trentham. Singing was led by the choir of the Outcasts' Music Society conducted by Alfred Pinnington.[10]

In the same period films were shown to CCH staff by the Ministry of Information on such varied subjects as the importance of growing your own food, methods of dealing with new types of fire bombs, and the siege of Tobruk.[11]

In the meantime, members of Siren Theatre continued to entertain not only at Trentham but also on tour. Productions such as 'Charity begins -' and the comedy 'Parcel of Mischief' written by member Joan Wilson visited local factories and the Loggerheads Sanatorium, the proceeds being donated to various local charities. Of such actions a contemporary edition of the house journal records *'their popularity and success all over the Potteries demands that tributes and acknowledgement should be made of their splendid efforts for war workers and charities.'*[12]

On 17th December 1942 a delegation of CCH staff, including the Comptroller, visited the North Staffordshire Royal Infirmary to present a gastroscope. Surgeon R.A.Keane commented that the hospital had 'long coveted such an instrument' (used for examining the interior of the stomach). On behalf of the establishment the gift was accepted by Dr E E Young who responded by saying that he did so with a *'due sense of gratitude and appreciation of the thought of temporary residents in the neighbourhood for the welfare of permanent residents.'*[13]

As Christmas approached the joint Editors of The Outcast observed - *'the incidence of wartime rationing will of necessity render feasting less sumptuous than of yore, but the spirit will surely triumph over the flesh!'*[14] However, parties were still in evidence at Trentham, but the main event was the well attended concert of Christmas music on 21st December in the restaurant.

As the year ended with the newspapers reporting that the Allies were *'going well on all fronts'*, the Mayor of Newcastle-under-Lyme, Alderman James Kelly, hoped that everyone could look forward to 1943 with greater confidence than when the shadow of war fell over the country - *'In quietness and in confidence shall be your strength.'*[15]

NOTES
1.	The Outcast Vol III pp9/47
2.	Ibid pp58 & 100
3.	Ibid pp1 & 113
4.	F.W.Hindmarsh op.cit p73
5.	The Outcast Vol III p134
6.	Ibid Vol II pp29/30
7.	Ibid p379
8.	Ibid Vol III P164
9.	Ibid p165
10.	Ibid p223 and Evening Sentinel 3rd September 1942
11.	Ibid p318
12.	Ibid p317
13.	Ibid p344
14.	Ibid p297
15.	Evening Sentinel 1st January 1943

Leonard Crainford

Chapter 9
Convalescents in the Park

'Adolf Hitler has, no doubt, quite unintentionally
done us one good turn. He has compelled us to bring in
a law which provides that every pedal cycle
shall carry a rear red light at night.'
Sir George Roberts, The Times 9th Sept 1939

As the war continued Stoke-on-Trent, in common with most areas of the country, shared the presence of wounded servicemen. Many of these arrived by special 'casualty' trains at Trentham Park station from whence they were transferred in convoys of ambulances, under motor cycle escort, to designated hospitals. After appropriate medical treatment, a number of these were removed to No 122 Military Convalescent Depot in Trentham Park, one of the largest such establishments in the country during World War II. The convalescents, together with numbers of hospital based wounded servicemen, were familiar sights in the streets of the city, and also at local events such as football matches, where it was not unknown for them to receive an ovation from the other spectators. Some can recall these servicemen visiting local factories, such as Josiah Wedgwood & Sons Ltd, whereupon as one person observed, the girls would 'tart themselves up' for the visitors!

Contrary to common belief, military convalescent units (or depots) were not merely a phenomena of the Second World War period. The idea appears to have been mooted as far back as 1909 and, having received approval in 1911 for units to be installed in time of war, the first were established in 1915.[1] Strictly speaking they were not medical units. They were intended purely for the reception of officers and men who required no further active medical or surgical treatment but who, whilst not yet fit for duty, were likely to be so within a reasonable period. The primary objectives of the units therefore were to *'hasten convalescence, to harden by graduated exercise under medical supervision, and to retrain its occupants.'* Another important aspect was that the units were intended to relieve pressure on general hospitals, particularly in times of emergency. Discipline and 'bull' were generally relaxed and 'irksome restrictions avoided' during the period of convalescence but, nevertheless, patients were expected to conform to the rules of the unit. If patients did not regain their fitness within a reasonable period, they were referred to a Medical Board.[2]

Interest in the use of Trentham Park for the purposes of a convalescent unit was first shown by the military authorities in late 1942. A team of officers from the staff of the Director of Medical Services, Western Command visited the site on 21st November to assess its suitability, two other sites already having been inspected earlier. Trentham became the preferred option - subject, amongst other things, to the provision of a gymnasium and other facilities which were deemed necessary. As a consequence, approval was obtained from the War Office as a matter of priority for the required works to be carried out at Trentham Park with a view to opening a 1700 bed unit in March 1943. Notwithstanding this, the first staff and equipment, including ambulances, were posted there on 21st December 1942.

It is difficult to define precisely who was responsible for the swift preparation of the site and the erection of the initial buildings. Times being what they were, records indicate considerable military movement in the area during this period, and it is thought likely that certain companies of Pioneer Corps, in conjunction with military engineers, were responsible for the preliminary works which included the erection of a number of nissen huts for accommodation of the convalescents. Later, however, No 122 Military Convalescent Depot was to have its own 'unit labour' for such purposes.

A number of subsequent inspections to assess progress at the Trentham Park site were carried out by, or on behalf of, Western Command's Deputy Director of Medical Services, Major General G.A.Blake, in early 1943. Records reveal that, whilst patients were now present at the camp, certain facilities including the gymnasium had not been provided by May, and that the Command's medical hierarchy, together with No 122 MCD Commanding Officer, Lieutenant Colonel J.Lawson, regarded such provision as 'acute'. There were further delays in that, by July, certain works at Trentham Park initially rated as urgent, had been put on a low priority level which resulted in representations being made to the GOC, Western Command, Lieutenant General E C A Schrieber. A subsequent visit on 14th October 1943 by Major General Blake, however, revealed that construction works, including the provision of the gymnasium, were 'well under way' so presumably the representations had effect! Furthermore, certain buildings including the kitchen and the NAAFI had been refurbished and the standards of the unit were reported as 'improving'. By this time the establishment of the units medical staff had also increased and included six Senior Masseuse. However, by the beginning of the following year the unit was being expanded to cater for 2000 beds and the Commanding Officer had been replaced by Lieutenant Colonel F B McKenzie.

Later that year, in the early hours of 6th June 1944, British and American airborne divisions were dropped into France, followed shortly after by seaborne troops. By the

81

end of the day - to become known as 'D' Day - some 156,000 had reached France. On 9th June the first special train bearing casualties from the new front arrived in the Western Command area via Birmingham. Whilst this in itself did not have immediate implications for convalescent units generally, the wounded being initially treated at general hospitals etc, nevertheless it is interesting to note that, by the beginning of August, concern was being expressed about the large number of convalescents which were arriving at Trentham Park. These were reported to include exhaustion cases which were arriving at a rate of 30 per week and which the Command Psychiatrist was 'dealing with'. By 11th August the convalescent depots of Western Command were under extreme pressure and reported as 'very full'. At Trentham Park a 'crisis expansion' situation arose which necessitated utilising marquee accommodation. As a temporary measure, however, it was arranged to transfer a number of convalescents to No.2 Military Convalescent Depot, Kingston but as a more permanent solution the possibility of utilising Stallington Grange, a substantial 19th century property near Blythe Bridge, as an annex was explored with War Office officials. By early October it was decided that further measures were necessary to ease the situation at Trentham Park, and in an effort to achieve this a block transfer of 200 patients to No.109 Military Convalescent Depot, Hamilton was arranged.

Resources in Western Command were even further stretched at this time with the arrival of 80,000 German prisoners of war, many of whom required medical treatment. Conflicting orders as to their dispersal caused much confusion for Command officials which merely added to the difficult situation. Furthermore, finding secure accommodation for the POW's, injured or otherwise, presented the military authorities with immense problems, the only solution to which, at times, was to transfer some elsewhere, including overseas. In addition, many of the prisoners were clad only in pyjamas which meant that they had to be provided with adequate clothing.

Having obtained approval for the temporary acquisition of Stallington Grange, it being deemed to be 'suitable for patients in the last stages of convalescence', concern continued to be expressed about the Trentham Park unit itself. Whilst recognising that it had been working at 'high pressure', particularly since the arrival of 'D' Day casualties, and that improvements were needed to the accommodation and facilities, it was finally accepted in March 1945 that the expectant capacity for the unit was too high and that a more realistic figure would be 1500 patients. Nevertheless, an inspection by Major General Blake during the following month found that the unit was 'running very well' although he noted that certain improvements were still required, notably enlargement of the kitchen and dining halls. In any event, use of Stallington Grange had by this time ceased, its accommodation having been found to be 'unsuitable' after all.

During the period that No.122 Military Convalescent Depot was stationed at Trentham there was close contact with the staff of the Central Clearing House. Joint events were arranged, notably by the units Sgt Major Reigate and Florence Hewson and Eileen Purcell of the CCH. These were well attended and appreciated by all concerned. In addition, convalescents attended CCH events and were made to feel very welcome.

convalescents marching to P T
They are pictured here
King's Wood. *E G Bull*

Some local residents still recollect seeing convalescent parties from No.122 unit undergoing training runs or walks at the rear of the park, and in the Hanchurch area. Ted Bowman, in particular, recalls instructors shouting to any lingerers - 'return to camp if you can't keep up!' Former Trooper Ken Webster (Northamptonshire Yeomanry) confirms the generally relaxed atmosphere at the Trentham unit. Recalling his period of convalescence there as a result of wounds received in Antwerp, Mr Webster agreed that instructors were 'sympathetic and easy' when conducting physical training sessions as they *'appreciated that their charges had experienced traumas of war.'*

On 19th May 1945, twelve days after the German High Command had signed an unconditional surrender of all its fighting forces, officials of Trentham's convalescent unit were ordered to inspect the former American Convalescent Depot at Stoneleigh, Warwickshire with a view to possible transfer. The layout was found to be 'first class in all respects' with accommodation for 3000 convalescents and staff. Other facilities included a large theatre, NAAFI, and sports ground with provision for massage, physiotherapy, education and occupational therapy. The state of repair of the depot was said to be 'excellent' with 'no RE work appearing necessary'.

As a consequence, immediate transfer of No.122 Military Convalescent Depot from Trentham to Stoneleigh was ordered, with 1700 beds to be provided initially. The Officer Commanding was also instructed to have an advance party in readiness, if required. By 11th July 1945, No.122 depot had completed its relocation to Stoneleigh, together with the 'overcrowded' No.123 unit from Witton Park, Blackburn. The combined unit at Stoneleigh was henceforth to be known as No.122 Military Convalescent Depot, that of No.123 being disbanded. Thus, yet another unique period in North Staffordshire's history, one which saw the presence of one of Britain's largest military convalescent units at Trentham, came to a close.

NOTES
1. Ex information R.L.Barrett-Cross.
2. Details of organisation of units from Army Medical Services in War (HMSO 1940) pp189/192
    All other details in this Chapter retrieved from PRO files WO166/6752 & WO177/258

Chapter 10
POW's

'The Nazis worship Might as Right - the Fascists do so too.
Both murder helpless citizens and persecute the Jew
Their outlook is just devilish, their code - mailed fist and gun;
Thank God 'blitz bombs' don't frighten us, or get us on the run.'
                                        P S Quick. The Outcast Vol I p322

The first German prisoners of war arrived in Britain in October 1939, being some of the crew of the submarines U27 and U29.[1] This created no major upheaval, the machinery for dealing with them having been established many years earlier. However, as more prisoners were taken, additional secure accommodation had to be found and this, in many instances, involved the hasty construction of special camps. As an alternative, the question of transferring German POW's to the colonies had been discussed in the House of Commons in 1940. This was said to have numerous advantages, the most significant of which was the removal of any likelihood of danger of the prisoners rising up and rejoining their units if Hitler's threatened invasion succeeded. As a consequence, large numbers were shipped to Canada, even after the threat had receded. However, in 1941, the Allies scored resounding victories in Cyrenaica taking some 130,000 Italian prisoners and these were brought to Britain. Of these, precisely how many found their way into Western Command is difficult to determine. However, records for the 1941-42 period do indicate a presence of 1500 Italian POW's from a batch of 8000.[2] With regard to German POW's, subsequent records reveal the presence of some 80,000 in that sector in October 1944.[3]

With a large proportion of Britain's able-bodied men serving in the armed forces, the Government turned to prisoners of war as an alternative source of labour. Commandants of POW camps were instructed to submit lists of 'reliable' prisoners who could be put to work and these were employed on various tasks such as agriculture, forestry and construction works.[4] The Geneva Convention laid down precise regulations in relation to the employment of prisoners of war. For example, under its terms, officers could not be forced to work unless they volunteered. However, the German Government had recommended via the International Red Cross that POW's be employed as a means of advancing their mental and physical well-being. Notwithstanding this, in many cases, German POW's remained reluctant, regarding consent to work as collaboration with the British.

Until the end of 1942 German U-boats had been sinking ships faster than the Allies could build them. The situation did improve to a certain extent but shipping, especially the North Atlantic food convoys, remained the prey of the U-boats. To counteract this, British gardeners under a gigantic Government propaganda campaign were urged to help beat the U-boat by growing more food. This was greatly assisted by the BBC's popular gardening expert, C.H. Middleton, who during his 'Dig for Victory' broadcasts, urged his listeners to grow potatoes, beans, and other vegetables as if they were munitions of war, just as surely as shells and bullets. Some seven million acres of grassland were put under the plough during the Second World War - even golf courses were dug up to grow potatoes and carrots in a bid to feed the British people. The Great Park at Windsor became Britain's largest wheat field and huge tracts of the Sussex Downs carried their first crops since the time of the Saxons. The Trentham Estate was no exception and by early 1940 areas were cleared, including the famous Italian Gardens, to grow vegetables. Reference to this is to be found in the following poem by Alice Eastern, published in that year:-

Where once the belles of the Five Towns
And many more besides
Roamed at their will, and danced with grace,
The Clearing House now bides.
Not only the inhabitants,
The gardens have changed too;
Humble potatoes lift their heads,
Where I admire the view.
Beside the stable courtyard steps
Flourish King Edwards fair,
And in the Italian garden
I found some growing there.
It seems the kitchen garden
Has spread itself around,
They've 'dug for victory' and food
The oddest bits of ground.
Last year the stately dahlia
Was flaunting its proud head
By sunlit wall. where now the leek
Grows happily instead.
And when the House is back in Town,
And Outcasts by the score
Go thronging through Post Office Court
As in days of yore,
The flowers will take their proper place
The dancers come again,
And the 'Beauty Spot of England'
Its title old regain.[5]

Italian POW's were employed in British agriculture from 1941 and they could be found working at Trentham from that period. German POW's did not appear there until 1944. Whilst the prisoners were not billeted on the Trentham Estate, some Italian POW's were eventually based on local farms. Otherwise, they were transported in daily, or as required, from their respective camps for work on grounds maintenance, the vegetable garden or farms on the estate, or those in the Trentham area. In the case of the Italians, the nearest camp to Trentham was at Tean (Camp No.134), whilst the Germans were at Madeley Tile Works (Camp No.193) or, alternatively, Shugborough (Camp No.99).[7]

Surviving records reveal differences regarding restriction of movement, methods of escort and guarding, etc. between Italian and German POW's. The Italians were treated, more or less, as 'trusties' even being allowed to walk up to three miles to their place of work. Perhaps even more surprising is the fact that parties of up to 12 were allowed to travel unescorted.[8] In complete contrast, the Germans were escorted everywhere under armed guard. Having said that, instances occurred when the British guards carrying out these duties had no ammunition for their rifles! Ken Webster, having spent a period of convalescence at Trentham, subsequently found himself guarding German POW's there with an empty rifle. He confirms that his charges were generally employed in keeping the camp tidy when not working in the fields locally. They also formed designs in stones outside the guard room etc for which competitions were held. Ken also recalls that during transportation of German POW's through Newcastle to Trentham, certain local females would jeer at the British troops and cheer and wave at their captives!

Both Mrs D.Beech and Eric Edwards recalled the Italians, in their brown uniforms with yellow/orange rings, working in the fields locally and on the Trentham Estate. Eric confirms that they were treated more leniently than the Germans. Many spoke a 'reasonable' standard of English and, according to him, they claimed to be 'happy working there' but 'detested Mussolini and the English winters!' Former 'Outcast' Mrs L.R.Pennell also recalls the presence of Italian POW's. At the time she was lodging in Wilson Road, Hanford and on cycling to Trentham Gardens daily, she saw a number, unescorted, proceeding to a nearby farm.

According to Miriam Kochan, at its peak Britain was host to some 402,000 POW's, confined in hundreds of different camps. Their official repatriation was completed in July 1948.[9]

NOTES

1.   Miriam Kochan Prisoners of England(Macmillan) p1
2.   PRO. WO199/409
3.   PRO. WO177/258
4.   'Reliable' excluded 'C'+ category prisoners (ardent Nazis)
5.   The Outcast Vol I p347
6.   F.G.Conti I prigionieri di guerra italiana (il Milino) p446
7.   Helmut Wolf Die deutschen Kriegsgefangenen in Britisher Hand
      (Verlag Ernst & Werner Gieseking, Bielefeld) pp129/132
8.   PRO. WO199/409
9.   Miriam Kochan op.cit p.vii

Chapter 11
Brylcreem Boys & the WLA

'I was held up by a passing Lancaster (or Wellington)!'
Contemporary excuse for late attendance at office etc when, during
the war, aircraft were frequently being transported into 16 MU for repairs.

The Royal Air Force, members of which were referred to as the 'Brylcreem Boys', first showed interest in land at Trentham Park in 1941 when the Superintending Engineer, Air Ministry Directorate of Works at Tunstall Hall, Market Drayton requisitioned 26.43 acres off Eccleshall Road. This was followed, some twelve months later, by a requisition of a further two acres in the same area and, finally, by that of Park Cottage on 2nd December 1943.[1]

The requisitioned property was intended for use as a Mechanical Transport Storage Unit (MTSU) for 16 MU, RAF Stafford. The Trentham Park unit was rated in the 'dispersed' category - a term being common to locations away from the main base, linked to the premise that the more dispersed assets were, the less likelihood of mass destruction by air raids. RAF Stafford had two other such units under its wing - The Quarry, Welshpool and Pottal Covert, Penkridge.[2]

16 MU itself had been formed on 1st December 1939 on an almost derelict builder's site near Stafford, following Treasury authorisation to purchase 362 acres of land. With a small number of staff its first Commanding Officer, Wing Commander W C Green MC, was placed under immediate pressure to bring the station up to operational status. Progress, however, was agonisingly slow, hampered by frost and heavy snowfalls. In fact conditions were so bad that the contractors, McAlpine, had to abandon work for almost six weeks. When the weather eventually eased, good progress was made with storage and engineering facilities being given high priority. The first serving airmen, in the shape of a Sergeant and four aircraftmen (cooks and butchers), arrived on 27th April 1940. By July/August, 500 airmen were under canvas at the station. However, by 1943, its establishment had risen to 4400 males and females. Supply and engineering functions formed the background of the station's role and included airframe and fabric repairs.

According to the authors of the station's official history, the first receipts and issues of equipment were in May 1940. By the following month the MT Squadron's activities and workload had increased to the extent that its vehicles were averaging almost 30,000 miles per month. It is interesting to note that, whilst equipment was being received by road and rail at Stafford, use was also subsequently made of waterways with the takeover of Penkridge Lock wharf. Whilst the station did experience the occasional air raid threat, it was most fortunate that it was able to continue its task of meeting the RAF's (and later, the USAAF) needs throughout the war, without too many interruptions.[3]

Winter 1941. CO's Parade, 16 MU, Stafford.   *RAF Stafford*

Records appertaining to 16 MU, Stafford are, perhaps, naturally biased towards the main station itself and there are few references to its satellites. Therefore, little information may be gleaned as to the precise functions or size of the MTSU's etc. However, the Trentham Park site was considered to be of sufficient importance to be inspected by Air Marshall B.G. Donald on 9th November 1943.[4]

According to a number of local sources the Trentham MTSU consisted of a compound with, amongst other things, 2 or 3 large sheds (or huts). Presumably, Park Cottage was used to accommodate staff. When the site was vacated by the RAF in 1945, it was taken over by the Women's Land Army for a brief period.

The WLA's establishment in 1944 stood at 80,000. It had operated on a smaller scale in the First World War but had been reformed in 1939. It was not really an 'army' as such. Nevertheless, its recruits came from all classes and they had to be mobile and work wherever they were sent to. They performed various functions but, principally, were engaged in agriculture and the production of food. Until disbanded, others performed important tasks as members of the WLA 'Timber Corps' where they were engaged in tree felling, working in sawmills, or selecting trees for poles and timber.

For many females it was an entirely new type of existence. The work was hard, often carried out in harsh weather conditions, but the practical clothing that was issued for tackling jobs such as tractor driving assisted in the wearing of trousers becoming more acceptable. Women have not looked back since!

NOTES
1. TE. Air Ministry requisitions
2. PRO. AIR24/903
3. Fifty Memorable Years - RAF Stafford 50th anniversary booklet
4. PRO. AIR 29/976

Chapter 12
The CCH - The Final Period

*'I'm not getting any new flags, I'm using an old one
I had left over from the last war!'*
Overheard on PMT bus during period of Victory Celebrations in 1945.

In charting the activities at the Central Clearing House during its final phase at Trentham, there is little to record. Primarily, this is because The Outcast magazine, the main source of information, ceased production in February 1943 as a result of 'pressure of changing conditions and personnel in the House'. However, it was the express wish of the Comptroller, Brian H.Bennett, that every attempt should be made to continue in some form a publication which would have *'the dual purpose of providing the present staff with a record of their activities and, at the same time, preserving a link with the past.'*[1] The result was the Outcast Observer, an eight page monthly, but it appears that few copies of this publication have survived.

Evidence does exist, however, that staffing continued to be a problem, with the establishment being increasingly reliant on local recruitment. For example, in 1945, from a total of 898, 619 were recruited from the North Staffordshire area.[2] In addition to this, there were ancillary staff (ie. cleaners etc) recruited locally. Consequently, it had been clear for some time that when the CCH returned to London, there was likely to be an adverse effect on the local economy. Moreover, the situation was likely to be further exacerbated by service personnel returning to the area and seeking employment.

In the final phases of the war whilst sporting activities continued at the CCH, it became more difficult to keep the Outcasts' Sports Club active. The reason for this was given as the departure of both male and female members to the forces, and the influx of hundreds of young females of around 14 years of age. Nevertheless, the club did remain active and it was a credit to the officials concerned that they maintained the various sections which continued to play such a great part in encouraging friendship and camaraderie not only amongst the different Banks in the CCH, but also with the many clubs in the surrounding district.[3]

Likewise, Siren Theatre continued to be one of the CCH's most successful ambassadors. Side by side with the main group, its Touring Players under Janet Halliday also gave performances at various venues in aid of charity. Precisely how much was raised by the 'Outcasts' during their period at Trentham would be difficult to calculate but it must have been many thousands of pounds, the majority benefiting local charities. Amounts are not always quoted in those documents which have survived, but in early 1943 alone one set of performances raised £250. Like the Sports Club, Siren Theatre was not so active in the late stages of the war period. For example, in the beginning, as many as nine different productions were staged annually at Trentham, or on tour, but by 1943-44 these had reduced to 5, with only 4 in 1944-45.[4]

Meanwhile the war in Europe was over with Germany surrendering unconditionally on 7th May 1945. This was followed, on 12th September, by the formal surrender of the Japanese at Singapore. As it happens, one of the earliest of the victory celebrations in North Staffordshire took place on 7th May with a huge bonfire in Trentham Park. On the following day the local Evening Sentinel heralded the event as 'a funeral pyre of Nazism' on account of logs for the blaze having been collected by German POW's!

Subsequently, when the victory bonfires had faded away and Britons had began to consider how they were going to rebuild their lives during the peace, discussions were held between representatives of the Bankers' Clearing House and Messrs Taylor & Humbert, agents for the Trentham Estate, regarding the termination of the lease of the Trentham Gardens Ballroom and the return of the CCH to London. It was mutually agreed that the tenancy should terminate on 16th August 1946.[5] Notice of the impending return was given to the staff by way of formal notice on 20th February 1946, together with terms of service for those who had been employed in a temporary capacity. Those for whom it was not possible to find permanent positions were given three months notice on 16th May 1946 and they were also notified that they would receive a 'leaving gratuity.' Some of the original remaining 'Outcasts' returned to London before August, their services being required there. In fact, the Outcast Observer in its final edition of June 1946 referred to some Bank sections as having began to look 'very thin' as regards numbers of staff. A few never returned to the capital, having married and decided to remain in the area. On the other hand, some employed in a temporary capacity, having married permanent members of staff, moved south. The final edition of the house journal lists numerous weddings and also the safe return of a number from the theatre of war.

From April 1946, life at the CCH appeared to be one seemingly endless round of parties and celebrations as staff prepared to leave for the capital, or left to seek alternative employment. The King's Hall, Stoke on Trent was the venue for the temporary staff farewell dance where Comptroller Brian Bennett was presented with an engraved silver tankard in appreciation of his kindness and consideration towards them. With dancing to the locally renowned Reg Bassett Band, the attendance was estimated at 1,250.[6]

Siren Theatre gave its final performance on Saturday 11th May 1946. The entertainment for the occasion consisted of scenes from eight previous productions, together with items from the repertoire of the Touring Players. It proved to be an enjoyable evening, tinged inevitably with regret for the passing of the popular institution. An invited audience of 450 attended. At the event news was given of Leonard Crainford who had laid the foundation of the theatre. Having left in 1942 to join CEMA, he had subsequently joined the Stratford upon Avon Festival Company as General Manager.[7]

Among the popular social events during this period was that given on Friday 31st May 1946 for the maestro himself, Alfred Pinnington, on the eve of his departure for London. Attended by the entire staff of Barclays section, the evening evolved from an informal reception to a formal Smoking Concert featuring artistes such as Dora Capey with whom he had been associated since his move to North Staffordshire. The high spot of the entertainment, however, was said to be the appearance of *'two stalwarts of the law'* who proceeded to *'disturb the peace with their mellifluous rendering'* of Offenbach's famous 'Gendarmes Duet'. Their thin disguises, however, were insufficient to hide the true identities of Pinnington himself and Comptroller Brian Bennett. At the conclusion of the evening Pinnington was presented with a Spode fruit bowl. In his farewell speech he said that he came to Trentham *'with certain misgivings, but was leaving with memories of the happiest days of his life.'* Although returning home, he frankly admitted that he had *'nothing but regrets at the parting from his many friends'*.[8]

Prior to the CCH closure those members of staff remaining took advantage of a number of coach excursions before returning to London. The destinations included Snowdon and Caernarvon, Blackpool, Rhyl, and New Brighton via Liverpool and the Mersey Tunnel. Whilst these gave much pleasure, those who participated in the New Brighton excursion were distressed at seeing the damage caused by bombing at Liverpool and of the obvious suffering of the residents. So came to an end the banking era at Trentham, an occasion which inspired the following lines:-

'To a new and different life we all
Too soon must go, but in the days to be
Where'er we are, we shall recall
The happy years, the comradeship
Of this portion of our lives, and so
Be glad that we, each in our different ways
Our parts have played. We have to go
But with us we shall take a memory true
Of work and play well done, of happy hours
Among green trees. To those our friends, we say
Remember us and Good Luck all the way.'   KB[9]

It is interesting to note that there appears to have been a certain amount of ill-feeling or resentment towards the staff of the CCH from a number of their colleagues employed in local Banks and at the Head Offices of the Banks in London. For what length of time this persisted, or how serious it was, is difficult to determine. However, according to a surviving document written by on the original 'Outcasts', there was an 'extraordinary impression' that the work at the CCH, Trentham was *'largely fun and games and that the staff had a relatively easy time'*. She goes on - *'never before the war was it ever said that the staffs on clearing work had an easy time or that their lot was one which was envied by their colleagues in other departments and it seems difficult to see how such an opinion could logically be arrived at when, during the past six years, an increasingly large number of cheques have been handled annually with not only a less total staff than at the end of 1939 but with a vastly changed staff both in the proportion of girls to men and in the average age of the employees.'*[10]

The writer of the document is quite correct as the following table, indicating the numbers of articles cleared, shows;[11]

	(Millions)					
	1940	1941	1942	1943	1944	1945
January	31.5	29.2	30.3	29.7	32.1	32.5
February	26.4	24.3	24.7	24.5	26.6	27.5
March	25.7	26.2	26.6	27.1	29.0	29.5
April	29.6	26.2	27.4	27.0	28.3	29.7
May	28.0	27.6	26.6	27.5	29.4	28.6
June	25.8	25.5	26.5	26.3	28.8	—
July	30.1	29.5	30.3	31.1	31.1	—
August	24.6	26.2	25.7	26.0	27.3	—
September	22.2	25.3	24.6	26.2	26.8	—
October	26.8	29.1	28.8	29.6	30.3	—
November	25.3	25.7	25.2	27.3	28.7	—
December	25.6	27.2	26.9	28.1	28.2	—
Totals	321.6	322.0	323.6	330.4	346.6	

Also from the same source, the following illustrates the composition of staff during the same period -

	Male	Female	Total	Local	London
January 1, 1940	363	592	955	123	832
1941	320	681	1,001	316	685
1942	268	719	987	466	521
1943	180	740	920	520	400
1944	172	725	897	567	330
1945	170	728	898	619	279

The first table gives an indication of the success of the CCH and its great contribution to the country's war effort by the number of articles cleared at Trentham, which rose from less than 322 millions in 1940, to well in excess of 346 millions in 1944. This was despite the fact that there was less staff than originally, and the establishment subsequently consisted of a different composition incorporating a large number of younger, inexperienced personnel who had to be trained. It should also perhaps be said that, whilst The Outcast house journal does provide an extremely valuable record of the CCH at Trentham, anyone reading the publication could, perhaps, be forgiven for gaining a false impression of life there, as little or no reference is made to its primary function which was, after all, a vital service performed under the stress of war.

NOTES
1.   The Outcast Vol III p365
2.   F.W.Hindmarsh op.cit p73
3.   Outcast Observer June 1946 p19
4.   Ibid p15
5.   TE. Letter dated 13th June 1945 from Bankers' Clearing House to Messrs Taylor & Humbert.
6.   Outcast Observer June 1946 p10
7.   Souvenir programme
8.   Outcast Observer June 1946 p3
9.   Ibid p24
10   Nancy Stafford Hines. Epic poem(unpublished)
11. Quoted by F.W.Hindmarsh op.cit p73

Saturday 5 January 1946. The first passing out parade for 164 OCTU.
Cadet Niven receives the Belt of Honour with Commanding Officer
Lt Col D L Darling standing to the left of the picture. *W P Crabtree*

Chapter 13
The Post War Period & the Officer Cadets.

*'You there - yes that idle cadet,
you are marching like a ruptured duck!'*
RSM Charles Cop, 164 OCTU.

In November 1945 yet a further friendly 'invasion' occurred at Trentham Park with the arrival of 164 Officer Cadet Training Unit (OCTU) from Barmouth. Whilst this was shortly after the war period it is, nevertheless, important in the history of the estate.

164 OCTU was one of a small number of infantry training units, whose successful cadets were eventually commissioned into infantry regiments. The units had been very much a special wartime venture designed to 'churn out' officers (or as one former cadet remarked - 'cannon fodder!') in an intensive 16 week course - 17 weeks including leave. Notwithstanding, at this period, young officers remained much in demand to replace those rapidly being demobilised. Prior to the course itself the cadets would have attended a War Office Selection Board (WOSB - known to one and all as a 'WASBEE'!). Generally, those attending at the selection process would have served in the ranks, but only one in ten would have experienced active service. The bulk of the units training was carried out within the confines of Trentham Park for which an additional 100 acres was requisitioned.[1] Otherwise, major exercises were pursued in North Wales, particularly at Dolgellau Battle Camp.

Under the command of Lt.Colonel D.L.Darling, 164 OCTU comprised 5 Companies - A, B, C, D and Headquarters. Each of these consisted of approximately 100 men, and newly arrivals initially joined 'D' Company. The establishment was well in advance of 800 personnel including training, administration and medical personnel etc and, on occasion, some famous names appeared on the units muster roll. For example, in the early 1940's, one platoon included cartoonist Roy Ullyett, composer Ross Parker - who, together with Hugh Charles, wrote 'There'll always be an England' and the actor Martin Wyldeck.[2]

The last 'passing out' parade at Barmouth was on 15th November 1945 after which Peter Crabtree recalls that he and his fellow cadets were sent on a 72 hour pass. During this period the move to Trentham Park was effected. All personnel were instructed to report to the new camp and Peter recollects his arrival at Trentham quite vividly. Having been met at Stafford railway station by army transport, being the only passenger for Trentham on his train, he was 'unceremoniously dumped' at the park gates on a cold winter evening, in complete darkness. The driver gave him directions to proceed along an unmetalled road which he did rather apprehensively, until a pinpoint of light was detected some distance away. This turned out to be a hurricane lamp outside a hastily pitched tent which was serving as the guard room! After following further instructions to continue along the same route, the lights of the camp Nissen huts became evident.

The camp accommodation had not been occupied since July, having been vacated by personnel of No.122 Military Convalescent Depot and, according to Peter, it left much to be desired. The heating and lighting were 'inadequate' and the beds 'damp'. As a consequence, he and his colleagues slept fully clothed for several nights in an effort to dry the bedding out. In addition, allocation of coal for the hut stove was 'insufficient' and consequently much of the their spare time was occupied in 'scrounging fuel'. Amongst other things, this involved raids on the adjoining area of Kings Wood which was expressly forbidden by the authorities!

In Peter Crabtree's case the firebrick lined stove proved to be unsuitable for burning wood, as the brick absorbed the majority of the heat. In an effort to remedy the situation, Peter and his colleagues therefore removed the lining which resulted in a warmer, cosier hut but which also soon proved to be detrimental to the stove. 'The base glowed red' he recalled, 'then almost white hot!' The apparatus, including the stove pipe, eventually collapsed, resulting in the whole place being covered with soot! A raiding party was hurriedly organised to replace the damaged stove with one from unused accommodation, and Peter and his colleagues then worked well into the night repairing the damage and clearing up the mess. Needless to say, next morning's inspection passed off without any problems, and no-one in authority appeared to notice the 'new' stove!

The first 'passing out' parade at Trentham involved 'B' Company, and this occurred on Saturday 5th January 1946. Participating in this event, like all other ceremonial occasions at the camp, was the awesome figure of RSM Charles Cop whose ever watchful eye never missed a trick! Cop was the second most senior RSM in the British Army at the time and, according to Colin McIntyre, he appeared to regard cadets as 'the lowest form of animal life!' 'You call me "Sir" and mean it' he would roar, adding 'I call you "Sir" because the army says I must!'. RSM Cop had a descriptive epithet rather than a name for each cadet, and his rhetoric was legendary. Colin McIntyre accepts that he was 'that 'orrible little Scotsman with a red feather!' - a reference to the red hackle of the Black Watch Regiment. On the other hand, Peter Crabtree recalls an occasion on parade when a cadet standing next to him had incurred the RSM's wrath. The RSM marched smartly towards him carrying his large pace stick held shoulder high in the horizontal position, only to stop when it's shiny brass point was approximately half an inch from the unfortunate cadet's nose. This proved to be too much for the poor fellow who, by now being in a state of shock had dropped his rifle, was put on a charge for 'casting away his rifle in the face of the enemy!' On another occasion, RSM Cop witnessed a cadet freewheeling past the guard room on a cycle. For this the rider was charged with being 'idle on a bike!' Likewise, a cadet fainting on drill parade would earn no sympathy from the RSM but rather a remark such as 'My God, that's disgraceful. Catch him Sgt. Major and put him on a charge for falling out without permission!'

At Barmouth the parade ground was only approximately 100 yards from the sea. As a result, RSM Cop frequently took great delight in parading his cadets at the double in the soft sand with rifles held in the air. On one such occasion when the RSM was giving his charges a rough time, the slight figure of an elderly lady appeared on the parade ground waving an umbrella in a threatening manner and hurling abuse at the RSM. Quite unmoved, he roared, 'Get orf my square, madam! Sgt Major, take this lady away!'

But, according to Peter Crabtree, RSM Cop was probably most famous for the occasion on which he marched a squad of cadets into the sea at Barmouth! However, having said that, Peter concludes *'when the RSM had finished with you, you could certainly drill, and when there were 100 cadets on parade moving as one, it made us feel very proud.'*

As with the French and other service personnel at Trentham, the officer cadets attracted the attention of certain members of the female population. According to Fred Powell, the cadets were extremely popular with the local girls who arrived by bus at Trentham Park 'tarted up and ready for the kill!' Unfortunately, the girls were not given too long an opportunity to pursue their quarries, as by July 1946 the unit was again on the move, this time being transferred to Eaton Hall, near Chester, the former seat of the Duke of Westminster. Prior to this, as might be expected, the cadets took the opportunity to share a number of social and sporting activities with the staff of the CCH. In fact, OCTU teams are included in the final fixtures listed in the house journal.[3]

After the departure of the cadets, the Trentham camp was occupied by units of the Polish Resettlement Corps. Yet again, this was only for a brief period, they eventually dispersed to camps at Blackshaw Moor, near Leek and further afield in Scotland. In any event, all land which had been requisitioned from the Trentham Estate for military purposes was surrendered by September 1947[4] by which time a sum of £10,500 had been negotiated and received from the Bankers' Clearing House for dilapidation, breakages, etc. arising from occupation of the Ballroom.[5]

NOTES
1. TE. Correspondence from HQ.,Western Command to Trentham Estate
   dated 6th February 1946.
2. Ex. information from Assistant Regt.Secretary, Royal Regt of Wales (24th /41st Foot)
3. Outcast Observer. June 1946
4. TE. Notice of Surrender from HQ.,Western Command dated 9th September 1947.
5. TE. Correspondence from Messrs Louis Taylor & Sons to Trentham Estate dated
   15th July 1947.

The Private Conservatory, Trentham c1880

Postscript

In 1974, following consultation with Elizabeth, Countess of Sutherland, officials of the Bankers' Clearing House in London decided to commemorate the 'wartime activities' of the Central Clearing House at Trentham. It was decided that this should take the form of a sculpture and Robert Berkoff was commissioned to undertake the work. This was formally presented, on behalf of the Committee of London Clearing Bankers, to the Countess by Sir Eric Faulkner MBE, Chairman of Lloyds Bank, at a special ceremony held at Trentham Gardens on 24th February 1976.[1] Official guests for the occasion included the Chairman of Staffordshire County Council (Councillor G.W.Newman), the Lord Mayor of Stoke-on-Trent (Councillor D.Shotton) and Mrs Shotton, the Mayor of Newcastle-under-Lyme (Councillor W.E.Welsby) and Mrs Welsby, and Mr R.F.Chatham who, as former Chief Inspector of the Bankers' Clearing House, had masterminded the transfer to Trentham in 1939.[2]

The Berkoff Sculpture, Trentham Gardens 1989, photographed before falling into disrepair.   *Author's collection*

Robert Berkoff's unusual work stands in the Italian Garden at Trentham and is described as 'representing the rim of a 50p coin showing the crests of the Banks of the time and enveloping embryo man'.[3] It was intended to convey the all-embracing concern of the Banks for the financial well-being of their customers. Sadly, its construction from glass reinforced plastic has not enabled it to withstand the rigours of the North Staffordshire climate and, at the time of writing, it is in urgent need of attention. It would be a tragedy if the work, which commemorates a unique phase in North Staffordshire's history, were to be lost.

The Trentham Estate is no longer in the hands of the Sutherland family, but in the ownership of British Coal. Sadly the famous miniature railway and swimming pool are no longer in existence but Trentham Gardens nevertheless continues to attract the public from far and wide who gain pleasure from its various features, including the famous ballroom.

As for the military camp, a number of the hut bases and fragments of overgrown foundations remain. Lengths of military roads and kerbing are partly visible, together with the square. Otherwise little remains, with the whole site returning to nature.

Ruins of the Military Camp, Trentham Park.   *Author's collection*

Finally, a 'legend' persists of the French servicemen having been responsible in 1940 for the wholesale destruction of Trentham's historic deer herd. This is reinforced by a further rumour that deer were 'reintroduced' to the estate after the war. There is no doubt that the French servicemen during their period at Trentham did slaughter a number of the deer, but it is extremely doubtful that the herd would have been completely eradicated. If any new deer had been introduced as thought, it is perhaps more likely that it was to reinforce the existing stock. The herd is still in existence and continues to thrive. Long may it continue to do so, together with the other fauna at Trentham.

NOTES
1. TE. Briefing note for media dated 24th February 1976
2. TE. Seating plan for luncheon following ceremony.
3. TE. Briefing note for media.

Trentham today   Author's collection

Bibliography

In addition to those works quoted in the source notes, I found the following particularly relevant:

Paul Auphon & Jaques Mordal.	The French Navy in World War II English translation	Sabalot Greenwood Press, Connecticut
M Gilbert	Finest Hour	Heinemann
P Cosgrave	Churchill at War Vol I	Collins
K Zbyszewski	The Fight for Narvik	Lindsay Drummond
J Colville	The Fringes of Power	Hodder & Stoughton
P&L Gillman	Collar the Lot!	Quartet Books
N Harman	Dunkirk-the Necessary Myth	Hodder & Stoughton
B S Johnson	The Evacuees	Victor Gollancz
B Wicks	No Time to Wave Goodbye	Bloomsbury
M Windrow	Uniforms of the French Foreign Legion 1831 -1981	Blandford Press

Abbreviations

In the text and source notes abbreviations denote the following:

CCH	Central Clearing House
APACS	Association for Payment Clearing Services
PRO	Public Record Office
TE	Trentham Estate records.